Independence Days

Cheers,

Independence Days

Still Just Boys and Other Stories

Justin Matott

Brewers Publications
Boulder, Colorado

Brewers Publications
A division of the Association of Brewers
P.O. Box 1679
Boulder, Colorado 80306-1169
303-447-0816; Fax 303-447-2825

Printed in the United States of America.

5 4 3 2 1

ISBN 0-937381-75-6

Library of Congress Cataloging-in-Publication Data

Matott, Justin.
      Independence days, Still just boys, and other stories / Justin Matott.
         p. cm.
      ISBN 0-937381-75-6 (alk. paper)
      1. Matott, Justin—Childhood and youth. I. Title.
CT275.M464446 A3 2000
814' .54—dc21

                                                                  00-064155

For Scott Ward,
through thick and thin,
"Cuz, we bros."

Contents

Prologue

Some moments in life are locked into memory for mysterious reasons that stay after other memories have long since faded. There are moments, which at the time may seem unimportant, that color all of the experiences that occur after them. Sometimes we can define the exact moment when we crossed over from childhood into the journey toward adulthood. But once that fuzzy line is crossed, we forever fluctuate between the child we once were and the adult we have become.

The gist of each story is as it happened. But as you know, in the retelling, a story can take on a life of its own. To protect the identity of several of the people within, names and perhaps locales were changed, though only slightly.

Acknowledgments

Thank you all for participating in my stories— Andy, Goodnight, "Murray", Joe, Scott, Jeff, Michael, Mike, Quent, "Spike" (my sincere apologies), "M.B.", Ronnie, Ron, Dad, Martin, Paul and Jerry, Rich, Gabriel Peters, "Fink," Mark, Steve, "Baldy-Paulie", Anthony, Papa, Alan, JJ and Ethan, and to Toni Knapp, my publisher, editor, and sometime consultant.

I want to be seen here in my simple, natural, ordinary fashion, without straining or artifice; for it is myself that I portray....I am myself the matter of my book.

—Michel Eyquem de Montaigne, 1533–1592

Independence Days

Sometimes I remember that magical night as though it was just yesterday; other times it feels like it was three lifetimes ago or that it happened to someone else altogether.

It was the Fourth of July during the mid-1970s and I was fourteen years old. On that sultry, electric, summer night I was to taste a little of the fruits of the future, some true rights of passage, and would find a key to unlock some of the secret codes of adulthood. In many ways, I was changed forever.

The morning started the same way as every other July Fourth in our countrified neighborhood of Skyview, named for the expansive Colorado sky. Early morning noises echoed from garages up and down streets that were named for planets. Soon the gala parade would wind through Venus, Mars, Saturn, and the entire Milky Way as neighbors sitting on lawn chairs in their front yards looked proudly on.

Children had spent hours decorating their bicycles. They wove crepe paper the colors of independence through the spoked wheels, attached playing cards to make the

crackle-snap sound when rolling, and added other adornments in an attempt to top of all the other entries in the
parade. Often the family dogs were dressed in some humiliating getup to match the fancy biked child they'd be trotting
next to in the parade.

Streamers, horns, and anything red, white, and blue
festooned the streets. Families gathered to watch their youngsters in the annual parade. Now that I was older, the little
kids looked so goofy trying to win the right to lead next
year's parade.

Until that morning, I had been in the Independence
Day parade every year since I could ride a bike. I had always
looked forward to the event and proudly joined in on the festivities with my dogs. But this year was different. My old Schwinn
Stingray with its bright orange banana seat and fashionably
high sissy bar sat alone in the garage. I was just too old to be
in the parade anymore. I was fourteen, after all.

Down the street, I spied a small group of teenagers
under the streetlight where we all used to play summer games
of hide and seek and kick the can. My brother, who only a few
years earlier had been in the parade himself, was now one of
the leaders of the teenage pack. I walked toward them with a
tinge of regret that my parents had no one to watch for in the
parade this year and wondered if my brother would send his
"little brother" packing when I tried to join their cluster.

A part of me wished that I was still running around
like the little kids, but a bigger part of me wanted to be with
the older kids, doing what they were doing—and that didn't
seem to include the games of our childhood.

☆

That night a group of fathers and several college men home for summer break huddled around a barbecue pit in a vacant lot near our houses, laughing and telling stories, an annual Fourth of July male bonding ritual. The division between the men and boys seemed like a thin line indeed.

I watched my father's face intently, his arm frequently crooking at the elbow as he lifted a bottle of beer to his lips, joining in on the frivolity. There was something primeval about the men gathering around the fire, sipping from their beers. As the spent cans and bottles collected in small heaps, the men's laughter grew more raucous. Those of us in the shadows yearned for our own stories of someday.

The acrid scent of smoky gunpowder filled the air. Brightly colored fireworks screamed upward from driveways lining both sides of the street as whole families ventured out into tidy front yards to join in the jubilation. We boys, the ones awkwardly wedged between childhood and adulthood, stood in the middle of the street holding pop bottles as far away from our bodies as we could, sending the pop bottle rockets skyward, thrilled with each explosion in the rapid fire.

Dogs who weren't cowering somewhere barked anxiously as the entire neighborhood went crazy. We struck matches to fuses to explode our assorted firecrackers, including the occasional M80 (reportedly an eighth of a stick of dynamite), obliterating a pop bottle or a dented canteen. The younger children gleefully played at the curbside with the little black tablet snakes, watching as they coiled and smoked. Women huddled in small groups, whispering while sipping their wine and 7-Up concoctions, a wary eye on the younger children.

One of my brother's friends decided it was time for us to start making our own tradition—that it was time we all grew up a little bit and experienced some things of our own.

3

We followed my brother and his friends, the same group of teenagers who earlier gathered under the streetlight. I felt great anticipation in the pit of my stomach, as I knew we were entering a new zone. I had started the day conflicted about my changing role in the tribe. Now I was among the older, wiser boys, not just a "little brother", but an actual member of the group. I felt so excited to be included. Once, I would have been sent back to the little kids' tables, and called a punk or a tagalong. But this year was different. This year I was accepted. My brother even seemed to look at me differently. Everything was changing.

One by one, we secreted away to a hidden place, pilfering the odd, unopened can or bottle left in the men's cardboard holders, putting them away for our own gathering. Soon we would join in an age-old ritual of stories told over a shared brew, though stolen and covertly, somehow the experience sweeter because of it.

As the night grew darker, we all worked out a plan to meet on my roof. Some to embezzle a pilfered smoke, some looking forward to an early kiss from one of the few girls willing to join in on our strange manly ritual, and all to watch the fireworks from two distant towns. But what drew us up there mainly were the mismatched six-packs of beer and the promise of our own party to resemble the one going on below us.

That was the summer I first really noticed the girls I had grown up with. They caused feelings to stir in me that I didn't totally understand, but I liked this change a lot. One girl in particular had captured my imagination, and I hoped she would join our rooftop party.

After climbing onto the pitched roof of my house, I sat in the crook of one of the eaves and sipped from a cold can of beer with several of the boys. I had never had a beer before, and the bitterness surprised me. I secretly preferred cola but continued to sip gingerly from the can as my friends all remarked with exaggerated "Ahhh"s and "Oh, man, that's good!" I turned away before anyone caught the grimace on my face.

Then three of the neighborhood girls, including the one with whom I was so secretly enamored climbed onto the roof. My stomach did a flip-flop when I saw her. I had watched her quietly on the bus to and from school that year, and as she walked past my house every day on her way to the horse stables. She had made my heart flutter wildly since the first day I noticed she wasn't just a friend's annoying sister anymore, but that she was becoming a beautiful young woman.

She chatted with some of the guys when she caught me staring at her. Suddenly she came and sat so close to me on the pitched roof that I thought she might have been aiming for my lap. She motioned for me to pass her my can of beer, which I did gladly. She drank deeply of it and then exhaled loudly. The sweet scent of beer and lip gloss crossed over me, and instantly my fireworks were internal. The reality that we were drinking from the same opening on the can struck me that it was as close to a real French kiss as I had ever known.

I couldn't keep from staring into her eyes no matter how hard I tried, and then I saw that look in her face—the recognition of mutual desire—I didn't have any idea how to proceed without making an entire fool of myself. Then she leaned in toward me and kissed me lightly on the lips, giggled, and crossed over the top of the roof to get a better view of the fireworks miles away. My insides turned to jelly and my knees went weak with infatuated love. I followed her to the other side of the roof and sat right next to her for the rest of the fireworks display, barely able to breathe.

The beer and that first kiss were forever to be sealed together in my heart and mind as a magical moment, a time of growing up. Now, whenever I smell berry lip gloss, I close my eyes and I am back on the roof as though no time has passed since that magical night. It was the summer when I got my first real taste of what it was going to be like to be an adult ... and I liked how it tasted.

★

Several nights after that forever Fourth of July, my family was grilling steaks in the backyard with Dad's garden garlic and chives. We roasted corn and had new potatoes and a salad from the garden. Set near my place at the redwood picnic table was a summer staple in our household, my father's beverage of choice: Beer. The long, thin aluminum can no longer held the same sense of mystery for me. I had tasted of its fruit and was still somewhat unconvinced of its total merit. I asked my father for a sip, hoping somehow to broach the subject of the drink he seemed to enjoy so much. He looked at me curiously and then handed me a half-drunk can and simply said, "Finish it ... if you like."

My mother flashed him a look. My older brother kicked me under the table. I assumed he was jealous that I had the guts to ask and wanted a swig himself. I took a long pull off of the lip of the can, raised my eyebrows in quick succession in my brother's direction tauntingly, and then grimaced visibly. My father smiled, looked at me, patted my leg and said, "It's an acquired taste."

Just then I noticed someone moving under the large cottonwood tree across the street where I had spent most of my summers in the tree house. It was *Her*. She caught my eye near the small barn where the horses found shelter several yards from the tree. The slight breeze carried her auburn hair as it floated and bounced about her shoulder like music. She crossed the pasture, coaxing her horse with an apple. She was carrying a bridle and grooming brush as I had seen her do so many times before. Soon she would be crossing the fields, perhaps down by the gently flowing creek, and then alongside the miles of stretching railroad tracks leading away from our homes. I thought about the kiss on my rooftop and wondered if maybe again …

She looked across the wide gravel road at me. Without a word, I knew she wanted me to join her. I asked to be excused from the table, and my whole family watched as I crossed the road, leaving from my yard as a boy and arriving on the other side a young man. I climbed through the barbwire fence and met her where she was brushing her horse down and I helped her saddle and bridle the horse. We rode together away from my house, me on the back, my arms tightly around her waist and breathing in the scent of her windblown perfumed hair. I wondered if anything in my life would surpass this moment.

Puppy Loves

Having grown up in a college town, once we boys got our own wheels we had license not only to drive, but also to crash college parties. College parties had two central themes pulling high school boys in like pheromones between two insects: one, beer; and the other, girls, girls, girls—and not necessarily in that order. We would slip into the dorm parties early in the year and mingle on the freshmen floor as though we were just hanging out because the crowd had gathered there. We would listen observantly to the freshmen complain about their class loads and specific class names and a few notorious professors, and learned to readily answer the usual questions: "What's your major?" and "Which dorm are you in?"

I was at an advantage, for I had been surrounded by the campus academia my whole life, as both of my parents taught there. Usually when asked, I would state my major as English and just complain about that salty old son of a gun professor Matott (my father), and where did he get off anyway? Other times when someone would push us hard regarding which dorm we lived in or to what fraternity we were pledged, we would make up something creative, often deferring to one of the other nearby college towns. If it got too obvious that we were just a gang of townies trying to scam some free beer or hit on the college girls, we would either move on to the next gathering or claim again more insistently to be from one of the other college towns.

★

On those weekend nights when a party for kids more our age was taking place, we would usually end up somewhere around the reservoir just west of town, to a cove nestled in the foothills overlooking the spreading town below. A great bonfire roared the entire night. Music blared from someone's car as a crowd gathered around, drinking from a keg, listening to the popular metal bands of the day—Aerosmith, Led Zeppelin, or Lynard Skynard. The crowd went wild with air guitars and raucous laughter, singing as "Free Bird" wailed on, symbolizing the freedom we all felt there. In retrospect, the freedom we truly had then.

The first time I felt as though I were really falling in love (a feeling that would recur to this puppy too many times) was across the bonfire at one of those parties during my junior year in high school. Susie Q. was beautiful; she had blond hair, a gymnast's body, and blue eyes that cut through the smoky haze like a knife. I watched her shyly and safely from my place with my buddies, wondering how I would ever bring myself to talk to her. How could I ever ask her out? She had only dated seniors since we were sophomores. A few times I thought our eyes had met in that certain way a boy and girl look at each other with mutual interest. I started to envision myself walking around the fire and taking her hand in mine as they did in the corny drive-in movies. We'd walk to a rock down by the water and kiss under the moonlight while our classmates unwittingly chattered on by the fire. She would tell me she had noticed me a long time ago at school and wondered what had taken me so long to ask her out. I would explain that I was afraid she would reject me. her head would tip back and she would laugh at how ridiculous that was. I would tell her that I'd watched her at school as she walked down the halls with her popular cheer-leader friends, that I had liked her the first time I set eyes on her. She would blush, appreciating the compliment, then reward me with a lush kiss. I would tell her how when she was cheering on our school's teams, I had always wished she were my girl.

There was something about the way the fire played off her cheeks and danced in her eyes that convinced me she was my destiny, this was our night. I found myself suddenly embold-ened, most likely by the beer I was gulping, but it was time to act. It was time to see what, if anything, would or could come of my consuming infatuation. I leaned over and told my pal my plan in confidence.

He looked at me incredulously. He started to shout something in my ear over the roar of the fire and the music; I could barely make out the words. "She's going out with a sen-ior, you idiot!" But in fact I knew that. I knew the heavyweight wrestler, her current beau, from our school was one of the toughest and meanest guys there. I had heard the rumors about them. They had just started going out. I refused to believe it. Hadn't my friend seen the way she was looking at me? Could that look be confused with anything but the same infatuated, lustful, searching, groping look to identify the con-fusing hormonal attractions that pull adolescents together unwittingly? He was just jealous. He just wished he himself had the nerve to speak to her or to one of her popular friends the way I was mustering the courage to do. But I was going to find out if there was any way she and I might somehow come together. I chugged the last half of my beer, popped a stick of gum into my mouth, and started to make my way through the throng of people who blocked my way as if to say, "Go back, don't do this idiotic, embarrassing thing." Bolstered by the challenge, the beer, and my long-standing attraction to her, I knew the time had come to let her know of my feelings.

Nearing halfway to where she was standing, I realized she had indeed been staring my way. I turned and gaped back where she was still gazing with that same longing, loving look, and saw that she had actually been looking right past me to where her new beau stood by the keg. She had a look meant for me still on her face, but she was oblivious of my presence. She no doubt was wishing he would return to her side and assist the fire in keeping her warm. My mouth hung open, my heart crushed in on itself, I wished for more beer. There wasn't enough beer in the keg to take away the crestfallen feeling that was building inside me. Someone started talking to me, and as though on autopilot I just answered, "Uh-huh."

Then a hand passed over my face, "Earth to Justin." I turned and looked at the pretty face of a girl I had taken out once but just didn't feel the same way about as I did Susie Q. "You know, she's not that great." With that she turned away and joined a cluster of her friends, who all looked over at me briefly and giggled in unison. Suddenly I was totally embarrassed. Had I been that obvious? Had it been that clear to the subject of my affection, too? Then I noticed she really *was* looking at me; this time there was no doubt. She smiled and mouthed, "Hello," and I thought I would melt on the spot.

As her newly found beau returned to his place beside her, enclosing her in a huge, gentle bear hug, I felt the night shift. No longer was my pursuit one of wishing on a star for her to notice me. No, it was time to lick my wounds and to join my other "single" friends in the pursuit of the perfect buzz, all trying to revel in the victories of our youth and to forget the defeats.

Still she *had* smiled at me that certain way ... maybe one more beer and I would take on the heavyweight.

☆

Another summer, another girl. We had been dating for months and I was totally enamored with her. She was surely the Real Deal. I took a road trip to California with two overly body-built guys for spring break and would—in the typical love-smitten, young, foolish, lovesick way—write her name in the sand with a stick and watch the ocean lap her name into its depths. My friends chided me mercilessly about my way of sending her a message, sans bottle. I anxiously awaited getting back home to be with her. We spent the evenings huddled around small fires on the beach eating beef jerky and drinking California brews. Though it was fun hanging out with the guys and sleeping sitting up, three in a small Toyota or on the cliffs surrounding Laguna Beach couldn't match the love waiting for me so patiently back home. The week seemed more like a month. Puppy love somehow translating the seven-to-one ratio in dog years to time itself.

The night we got back, there was a huge party that I planned to attend with a couple of my friends. I knew she would be there and wondered how long I would stay true to hanging out with the guys and our plan for simple reverie before cutting out with her. As we entered the party, some of my friends acted strangely toward me and tried to guide me off of the porch. I stood on the porch looking into the plate glass picture window and saw what they were trying to help me avoid. In the living room was my girlfriend, not only sitting on another guy's lap, but also kissing him. I became enraged and my pals pulled me off the porch as I yelled, threatening to kill him. Apparently the seven-to-one ratio of puppy love years worked on her, too, and a week was simply too long to wait for me. (So much for the Real Deal, eh?)

My friends pushed me into a car and drove off with me kicking and cursing them for not letting me take my revenge. Instead we drove around town looking for another party while I cooled my heels. We picked up some 3.2 beer and drove around some more. I pounded down the beer in the aluminum cans like it was water and remember waking up next to two of my friends in a strange backyard, fully clothed on the top of a trampoline. My head felt like it would burst (along with my heart), and the bright sunshine burned like a curse. Right then I wasn't sure which hurt more—my wounded ego and broken heart or my head complaining of overdoing the antidote for heartbreak the previous night.

I soon learned that my girlfriend (Miss Real Deal) had found our relationship to be moving too far too fast. She was just one of those heartbreaking puppy loves that would ensure I would be a wiser man for the woman sure to come into my life some day. And of course there would always still be more summers, buddies, and beer.

My experiences mirror those of thousands of others trying to grow up too fast. Puppy love is the practice that makes perfect, though perfection is a lofty goal no one achieves in the odd dance of men and women. Puppy love teaches hopefully more than just how to be, but how not to be. Few people would be willing to go back and relive their adolescence. There are so many reasons why this is true. It may just be puppy love, but it's always the Real Deal to the puppy.

The Village Idiot

One carefree night during summer break after my first year in college, my older brother, Martin, had a garage party at our parents' house. Early in the afternoon my best friend, Scott, and I helped him roll a keg of beer into the garage and tidy up the place. Martin invited all of his friends. One of those friends was Spike, who had been known in our neighborhood as the village idiot when we were children. He was the one who all the others sadly picked on and the kid who would do virtually anything on a dare, just to feel as if he belonged. His parents were both first-generation German immigrants, and their house always smelled of sausage, schnitzel, and strudel. His father barked in a rough, angry voice that you could hear for miles. Spike was awkward, strange, and foreign-seeming and unfortunately too often the brunt of every joke. My brother, however, formed an early friendship with him, often defending him when the other kids were unusually cruel, and they had stayed friends through all of it.

That night at Martin's party we all enjoyed the late summer heat and sipped from foamy, watery beer in plastic cups. I leaned over a table and asked our childhood puppet friend, Spike, what the new, rather large homemade tattoo on his forearm meant. He looked me straight in the eye, then he looked upward as if trying to recall something that just wouldn't come back, and earnestly said simply, "I forget." The tattoo was a giant, blackish-blue British cross, which he explained he had drawn with his hand and then marked permanently on his skin by repeatedly sticking himself with a fountain pen. I wondered why someone would brand himself and so crudely and how he could then forget the relevance of it. But as I had always assumed, Spike was simply one French fry short of a Happy Meal. At that point Spike became fair game for more pranks, the same juvenile types of pranks we had played on him a decade or so earlier.

★

As children we had convinced Spike of many ridiculous fables just to torment him and to provide us with a good laugh (I admit it—we were awful). Some of the more famous stories included that I was an experimental child astronaut on the first moon landing, that my brother had built the house we lived in, and that we collectively had invented numerous things—Hershey syrup, the trampoline, and other assorted fictions. He always bit hook, line, and sinker. Incredible as it seemed, he really believed us. As we all grew older and more cynical, somehow he stayed childlike in his innocent faith and belief in our stories. Once we convinced Spike to play "fish in the pond," wherein we would cast our fishing lines down into the driveway from the high point of our roof and try to catch him like a fish. He was willing to play along with the game. I cast my line downward several times; his job was to tug on the line, mimicking a fish. On one of my casts I felt the weight of a big "catch." A bloodcurdling scream came from below. I was initially proud of Spike for taking our game so seriously, then began to berate him that fish didn't make sounds like that, or any for that matter.

When I peeked over the eaves of the house, Spike was down on all fours begging me not to pull on the line anymore. My brother shouted something loudly at me, and I realized I had caught Spike right on the eyelid with the hook. My mother rushed out of the house, thinking someone was dying, and painstakingly removed the hook out of his eyelid with tools from her sewing box. I remember feeling shame when we walked him to his house and explained to his mother that it was an accident, without mentioning that her son was a fish. We were the real-life Eddie Haskells in Beaver Cleaver's neighborhood, able to put on a great front for his parents but acted like real shits when they weren't looking. But Spike's mom always fed us something delicious and unusual in spite of the fact that we weren't good to her boy.

Our favorite prank on Spike was an ongoing one my brother and I pursued together. We convinced Spike for several years that we possessed special warlock powers. Martin would always be in cahoots with me, me being the ringleader of the "warlock club." I would cite some bogus incantation, giving Martin verbal cues as I convinced Spike that by saying whatever silly thing I said, I could make things move or levitate. I would say something and my brother would secretly make it happen, usually from underneath our trampoline. Spike simply never caught on no matter how many times we did it to him. He was so convinced that we were warlocks while we were growing up that he would do anything to be initiated into our warlock club.

Initiation included whatever strange activity Martin and I could think of on the spot. To join the warlock club, Spike would have to go streaking through the entire neighborhood, drink disgusting concoctions we would combine in our mother's blender, or sing at the top of his lungs under the streetlight at midnight next door to the crankiest old man in our neighborhood. Spike would inevitably get caught, and the old man would walk him down to Spike's house to deliver him to his sleeping parents. It would get Spike grounded for an unusually long time. One round of warlock club initiation required him to hand a found prophylactic to the meanest neighborhood b-with-an-itch woman ever to walk on two legs, and asking her to try it on for him. Mrs. Rickley pulled him into her house by his ear and spanked him so hard you could hear him screaming out in the road with her door shut.

(Mrs. Rickley was seriously the meanest person I have ever met. It was she who exiled more than one boy's dog to the dogcatcher and kept any ball that might accidentally roll into her yard. Mrs. Rickley, wherever you are, it was me who broke your son Robert's watch, hung an entire box of blown-up prophylactics in your pine tree, trampled your corn a week before harvest two years in a row, and left all those bags of burning dog crap on your front porch and various other endless pranks, heh, heh heh.)

We waited there to see if Spike would ever come out alive, and soon his father came storming up the street to retrieve him. Numerous angry German expletives flew from his mouth, all the while he whacked poor Spike on the back of the head down the street. You could hear Spike getting a beating inside his own house and it would be another week again before we saw Spike outside after school. Other initiation included causing general mayhem in the still of the night that involved streaking and some of my mother's undergarments (which we inevitably made sure Spike was caught at). We would require that he bring tasty treats to my brother and me from his refrigerator or pantry, including a can of Hershey syrup (which, you'll recall, my brother and I had invented), to share and guzzle until the entire can was gone. The funny thing was, just when Spike started to tire of the initiation, we would convince him—using the same secret ploy—that he was making things move, too, albeit only apprentice-level stuff. We promised he would be a full-fledged warlock in no time, assuming the tasty treats kept coming.

☆

I was now in college and told Spike I wanted to initiate him to a fun fraternity house gag. He agreed to be party to it, probably assuming we had all grown up and out of the need to abuse each other. I began to explain the basic trick as I pulled a funnel down from my father's workbench shelf and told Spike as seriously as I could to place it in the front of his pants. Spike looked at me dully, suspiciously, surely waiting to see if I had matured any at college and wondering if he could trust me. I was tempted to recite some warlock incantation just for old time's sake but knew it would put him off.

I pulled a quarter out of my pocket and told him to place it on his forehead and close his eyes. He gauged me suspiciously again. Rolling my eyes theatrically as though deeply offended by his distrust, I showed him what I intended. To demonstrate, I placed the funnel in my own pants, put the quarter on my own forehead and without looking down but straight ahead the quarter fell into the funnel. I assured him that was all there was to it. I told Spike that I had practiced this trick for a long time and very few people could do it their first time. Further, that very few people were coordinated enough to do it at all, and if he could I would give him some kind of prize. My brother looked over at me and shook his head knowing I was up to something no good. Martin's face was a mixture of amusement and disgust at what he was sure was a mean prank at his friend's expense. I was tempted again to make a warlock joke or to remind Spike of the rubber he gave to Mrs. Rickley but held my tongue.

Spike looked at me again, still very suspicious, and slowly placed the funnel into the front of his pants. He kept looking at me cautiously as I feigned disinterest. Finally, he placed the quarter onto his forehead carefully and closed his eyes. I talked him through it as though he was embarking on a new sport that would require much skill. As he began to lower his head, eyes still tightly shut, I poured a full cup of beer (his, which he had handed me to do the trick) into the funnel, wetting the entire front of his jeans, instantly appearing as though he had lost all control of his bladder.

Startled, he jumped back, the familiar hurt betrayal in his eyes, which always made me realize again what a real shit I was but never stopped me from trying to get a good laugh. The other party-goers erupted in laughter and then shortly Spike joined us, finding it somewhat humorous, too. He thumped me on the arm and said, "That's a good one, huh? I'll remember that one." I felt slightly guilty that my mean trick had worked to make Spike feel like he was more a part of the gang again and that somehow the trick had initiated our friendship once more as far as he was concerned. It saddened me momentarily that I had taken advantage of one so vulnerable, but unfortunately (for me) the moment passed quite quickly.

About a half hour later, after my conscience had dulled with a few more kegged beers (and I swear this is true), I walked up to him, apologized again, and said, "Spiker, my old buddy, good friend, I really do want to show you how that fraternity prank works. For real this time, okay?" He again looked at me with total distrust and great skepticism. I remarked that is was almost impossible to get the quarter to fall from your forehead into the funnel, that if he could do it without looking down I would give him a twenty-dollar bill. I flashed the money. He frowned, sizing up the possibility. He looked to my brother, who rolled his eyes and walked over to the keg shaking his head, leaving the scene of the crime. Spike agreed, asking me if I really would give him the twenty-dollar bill if he could do it. I nodded.

Spike put the funnel into his pants, scoured the crowd with his eyes as if to say, "Look at me. I can do this on the first try." He hesitated, looking at me again as though wondering if I really would come forth with the twenty-dollar bill. I nodded as my brother's friends watched, half amazed at my audacity, half-amused by the scene. Spike incredibly tilted his head back, placed the quarter on his forehead, shut his eyes tight as I again baptized him with his own beer, flooding the crotch of his pants yet once more.

I quickly shoved the twenty-dollars into his front pocket and made for the front door of the garage as fast as I could. Scott and I erupted in laughter and jumped into Scott's car as Spike came barreling out the front door. I yelled "Hey, Spiker, nice cross!" referring to the homemade tattoo about which he had forgotten the significance and would wear the rest of his life. He shook his fist at me and yelled something I didn't quite catch as we roared out of the neighborhood, laughing hard at our own meanness.

★

Later on, after hilariously recounting the prank over and over while shooting pool at the Library, a local watering hole, my friend and I returned to the scene of the fraternity prank crime where the party had died down. As we crept into the now mostly quiet house, we saw that Spike had passed out on the couch, his crotch still slightly darker than the rest of his jeans. My brother sat upright, half-asleep in the recliner across the living room with his girlfriend and watching us as we slunk across the floor.

"Let's try that trick where you dip his hand in a bowl of lukewarm water on Spike while he's sleeping and see if he pees his pants for real," I whispered loudly. Martin and his girlfriend shook their heads and started to laugh quietly. Scott and I grabbed one last beer from the keg and went downstairs to watch the late movie. After we were sure Martin and his girlfriend had left or had fallen asleep, we started upstairs to retrieve the empty popcorn bowl for our friend Spike's hand baptism.

☆

Now, from the perspective of adulthood I realize that the village idiot was never Spike. Preying on the vulnerable and finding humor in berating someone who just desperately wanted to be my friend—though I cannot imagine why he would deem us worthy of his friendship—was the lowest of lows. If I knew where Spike was now, I would give him a heartfelt apology (and maybe an official warlock club certificate complete with a bronzed prophylactic) and let him know who was truly the village idiot. It was *me.*

Glory Days

Autumn often brings to mind the past, reminders of change, and times gone by. It heralds the end of summertime fun, summertime boredom, and of new experiences to come. When the first tinge of crisp air strikes, the boys of summer put away the baseball bats, mitts, and dreams of homeruns and start thinking of balls spiked in the end zones and crowds cheering on the boys of the gridiron. With the first nip in the air, my mind always reels back to the first days of school and of the football games in the neighborhood.

On the weekends we boys would play rough and tumble games of football in the early morning frost-touched grass at the City Park in the center of our bucolic college town community. One or two fathers would usually coach, and we all fancied ourselves a Joe Namath, Fran Tarkington, or James Brown: little weekend warriors with the desire to make an end-to-end touchdown or at best a bone-crushing tackle that would be appreciated by our teammates. Near the park's fields was an old-fashioned diner where a jukebox played "Cherokee Nation" or a popular Sonny and Cher tune over and over. We would gather there after games for the congratulatory pep talks and camaraderie, or for more coaching regarding our defeat.

We were only ten years old and as time ticked on, our teammates would all end up in different schools. But when we ran into each other, even many years later, we would remember the bonds that had formed on the gridirons of yesterday. Each winning play took on more and more detail and victory in our heads as we all, mostly all, realized that we were never to be a Joe Namath or a James Brown, at least not in football.

☆

As my present-day chums and I drive through the neighborhood shortcut to the stadium where we will see our first regular season football game, the radio blares with predictions and interviews regarding the upcoming game. Children run and play the games of autumn in a tattering, mismatched assembly of shoulder pads, helmets, and other game gear they have pulled together to imitate their gridiron heroes.

I remember again the ragtag crowds of boys who used to gather in my boyhood yard to play, and think of how my own boys do so now as well. Assorted football games have erupted on every street, emulating the heroes gathering in the stadium just north, the motion of the runners sweeping aside the fallen leaves that have accumulated on the ground. Young toughs, wishing to share in the victory of a spiked ball, a touchdown, and the respect of their pals just like we had when we were kids.

I want to jump from the car and join them, and then think of the last time, just a week ago, when I played with my own boys on our lawn and nursed my aching muscles and back in a hot tub for days as a reward. It wasn't so long ago that all of us "boys" met at an elementary school for a game of touch football. All that "touching" left us all mostly stooped over and rubbing sore muscles for the next week. I imagined if we did stop and challenge the young toughs to a game, "old guys against the young," how embarrassing it would be to call our wives from the hospital with the report that a vagrant band of ten-year-olds had sent the lot of us to the hospital with sprained ankles and concussions.

Soon we will be high-fiving the victories and the plays (albeit of someone else, rather than us), the crowd will erupt in the wave or a simple unified groan, or a cheer will erupt depending what is happening down on the turf.

The air has the distinct autumn crisp to it, a breeze kicks up, swirling the newly dropped leaves along the streets and I remember the early days of college when all was new and campus buzzed with excitement. The electricity of a new season, the anticipation of the impending holiday gatherings captures the imagination and causes an excitement I always wish could somehow be bottled. Soon the sultry days of summer will be replaced with the sprinkling of snow and then the ground will set hard for another season of winter.

We pass the many tailgaters as we head into the stadium, all enjoying celebratory beers, the football game beverage of choice. Music flows loudly from speakers set upon rooftops of cars and trucks. The smoke from barbecues peppering the air makes us all rub our stomachs hungrily as though on cue. Kegs are set in the back of pickups, and cases of various brews and a general festive, good-natured camaraderie abounds. Even when a brave soul happens across the sidewalk with the opposing team's jersey, most comments are in good taste and good fun.

Whether a college football game or a professional game plays to tens of thousands of spectators in the large stadium, the crowd buzzes with the same excitement, bleachers with plaid blankets and cushions, and the occasional thermos spiked with reinforcements from the cold foretell of cooler days soon to come. The band booms down on the field at half-time, the cheerleaders parading about in anticipation of another year of leading the school or hometown crowd in a frenzy. We are alive! We are young again!

As my buddies and I slap high-fives and look forward to an afternoon together away from work worries, children's squabbles, and "honey do" lists, someone suggests a cold beer. As though Pavlov himself has rung a bell, we all start to salivate again on cue. And then, serendipitously, the sound of the beer hawkers begins like a symphony; the celebration of the season is upon us. Soon we are clicking plastic cups together and cheering on our hometown boys. We will repeat this ritual every week for the cooling months to come, whether in the stadium or in front of the television.

Somehow this is how we men often learn to bond, to communicate with one another. We have our occupations, our pastimes, which we share without the need to discuss "why" too much. It is our strange way. After all, we are from Venus, or is it Mars? I'll never get that straight. Our language of high-fives, belching, and off-color jokes somehow say, "I understand," "I'm with you." And about the time the conversation could go deeper, a team scores and we are all pulled once again vicariously into the competition. All of us transfixed on our gladiator heroes down on the turf—somehow convinced deep down inside that had we worked just a little harder, been just a little bit more gifted, and wanted it just a tad more, that we, too, could have been a star. Somehow with time passing, our youthful victories have grown larger in our minds; we were all somehow a little faster, a little tougher, and a lot more talented than our friends remember us to be. But then, that's why they are called our glory days.

Bread Pudding and Dickens

When I was a boy, I would buy fifty-cent paperback comics. One of my favorites was "Andy Capp." Andy was a Scotch-plaid, hat-wearing gent with a propensity for the drink. He would stumble home to Flo after a night of drinking pints in the pubs of England with his friends. Maybe that was when I first became enamored with the idea of a place where guys could go to spend time away from life's issues. Kind of like a grownup version of the tree houses and forts my friends and I once built.

My chance for an Andy Capp experience came several autumns ago. I traveled to England and France with a client representative from the States and my team of seven from work to uncover new opportunities between our two companies. One of my co-workers, my technical specialist, Joe, and I planned to take the old saying "Work hard and play harder" to a new level in the playgrounds of London and France. In addition to "giving our all to the company store," we intended to sight-see, spend time with our spouses, and search for the perfect pub.

Joe and I wanted to experience the social aspects of male bonding and beer, famous there and lacking in most of the watering holes back home.

I anticipated beers "pulled" and cascading and the deliberation of the pubtenders, reportedly worth the visit to England's pubs alone. I specifically looked forward to the famous pulled Guinness stout. I mentioned to my cohort Joe that we should have a Guinness as our inaugural brew upon arriving in London, to which he sneered and made some such claim that he would not be drinking stout with me, thank you very much. If he wanted to drink oil, he would simply do so!

I surfed the Internet, looking for pubs and information about our London search for the ultimate pub. The day we arrived in London—before our American client, Joe, our spouses, and I were to meet our English clients—we set out to sight-see and "pub crawl." I stood under the eaves of a small shop not far from Piccadilly Circus, shielding myself from the drizzle that seemed so much a part of the fabric of the city. As I waited, I felt a slight drip on the top of my head and then another as it coursed its way down my hair onto my scalp. I reached up to smooth my hair out and was met with a sickeningly wet, sticky gray blob. I had been standing under several pigeons. My wife and friends began to laugh, when a rather distinguished looking gentleman stepped up to tell us in his wonderful English accent that actually I was the lucky one of the group. Folklore held that a visitor who was shat upon by a pigeon in the city of London would experience luck in the days to come. More interested in finding a way to clean the "luck" out of my hair, I popped into the shop and used the restroom and then we were on our way again.

We came upon a pub, the outside of which was shaped like an enormous bottle, and decided to go in and quench our thirst. We were in London to experience the beer. Humankind, more specifically men, had for centuries enjoyed beer as the conduit to good conversation and enjoyment. Even the Pharaohs had beer interned with their bodies as they passed from this life into the next. By the standards of the other pubs we would soon enjoy, the bottle-shaped pub was a dive.

We finished our pints and then moved across the street to a more bustling, cavernous pub, where we would get our first taste of pub food. We stood inside the wood-paneled pub taking in the culture of the environment. People murmured in private conversations while a few boisterous groups smoked and gabbed by the bar. My wife, Andy, made a comment about culture being in theaters rather than in pubs. It was then I knew that my pursuit of the ultimate pub wasn't worth explaining further. Though I was enthusiastic about taking in the sights, theater, and other aspects of London, I had hoped pub crawling would be enjoyed by all parties. Later, Joe's and my overstated comments about the perfect pint (my idea was the chocolate foam on a pulled stout, his a full-bodied India pale ale or lager) and the difference in body between the pints we were sampling drove our wives back into conversations about castles, princes and princesses, and the romantic countryside of England.

The next afternoon, I sat in a dour hotel conference room in a business meeting, my mind wandering to all that awaited us on the tourist circuit. After our meeting, Joe and I began to encourage our wives to go to the countryside to see more castles, hoping it would enable the two of us to hit a few of the old pubs near the London Tower before dinnertime.

Now my American teammates, our British counterparts, and our client headed out to some of the pubs near the tower along the River. The thick English cockney and other regional British dialects swooped about us as the bustle grew louder toward sundown. The aura of the pub, at first alien to us, the murmuring, the pairing of a few men here and there, and small gatherings of others drew me in and made me long for something close to a "local" pub back home. This was the ultimate in male bonding. I envisioned locking arms with the burly men in the bar in a rendition of an old English drinking song. We would throw down large tankards of dark brew and sing "God Save the Queen." Instead I just watched and listened and enjoyed the quiet, civilized conversations taking place about us.

Later at yet another pub after we rejoined our wives, I stepped up to the ornate bar to order for my group gathered at a large table and noticed that the pubmaster was not tapping the beer but was pulling it deliberately and with style, leaving a cloverleaf atop the foam of each glass. The carbonation mixture and the temperature, he explained, are what make such a difference in the body and taste of the beer. He asked if I wanted stout. I looked across the ornate handles on the pumps, names I had not known before, and asked for two Guinnesses, fully knowing that if Joe wouldn't drink it, I certainly would.

The pubtender pulled about half a glass in each of them and then set them on a shelf near the pump handles. As my hand reached toward one of the glasses, his eyes intently indicated to me that they weren't ready. I watched as the creamy froth cascaded in a dark and light variegated mixture, as though with a life of its own. He then held the glasses under his pulling mechanism again, finishing them off with his signature three-leaf clover atop a creamy half-inch of chocolate foam. It continued to cascade and then he motioned to me with a friendly nod to take the glasses.

I rejoined the group of ten at the table. The women were pacing themselves until dinner with pints of milder brew. I placed the stout in front of Joe. He sneered as though to say he wouldn't be partaking. I expected him to step to the bar and order a lighter beer, perhaps amber or even a porter, but instead he watched me as I lifted the glass to my lips and took my first sip. My mouth watered as if awaiting a delectable morsel. The beige foam clung to my lips and I could do nothing but exalt the incredible flavor. Joe looked at me suspiciously as though I were conning him to down something not fit for consumption, but then gingerly raised the other glass of stout to his own lips. As the glass came away from his face, I saw the same inexplicable gesture of pleasure that must have been evidenced on my own. The first sip had convinced him that he would be drinking stout for the duration of our trip.

☆

Ornate Christmas decorations were hung in lobbies and storefronts all over London. The chill in the air reminded me of the settings often surrounding one of my favorite British writers, Charles Dickens. I had always been enamored with Dickens and his era, and always wanted to spend a Christmas in old London to capture even a glimmer of what Dickens was so inspired to write about. Several nights later, I determined to follow along the paths Dickens had frequented.

As we sat in the pubs where Dickens was reported to have whiled away time, I imagined much hadn't changed over the past few hundred years. I looked to the corner of the room and pictured a man inspiring the character of Ebenezer Scrooge sitting lonely and terse while sipping from a bowl of gruel. Several children ran along the streets and I wondered if Oliver Twist might have favored these streets while pick-pocketing from the gentlemen in their fineries returning from a pub, slightly less aware. I watched the boats milling up the Thames River and thought of David Copperfield and his adventures here. I was sitting in an old pub where Dickens had sketched his ideas to write about and I pictured myself traveling backward in time and observing the very things that had inspired him.

My English counterparts offered to take us Yankees for a real pub crawl. When I mentioned that I would like to stay on London's East Side and have a Dickens tour of the pubs, they were delighted to accommodate. Seven of us walked from our hotel right across the bridge from the Tower of London to "the oldest riverfront pub in England" on London's East End. As we entered the hallowed Prospect of Whitby, we were immediately aware of the span of years it had been in operation.

The pub itself dated back to the time of pirates, and many other famous and infamous people had passed through its doors. We were in the area near Hangman's Noose where prisoners sentenced to death would swing and then their bodies would be lashed to the piers of the river and left until the tides came in and covered them. Jack the Ripper had stalked the very streets outside the pub and possibly found a few quiet moments in between his terrors on the same bar stools where we sat.

In England many years ago, pub-goers carried their own ceramic cups with whistles baked into the rim or handles while frequenting pubs. When a refill was required, the pub-goers blew into the whistle confined in the handle to get better service, thus the saying "wet your whistle." Also, those beer brewers in past times would dip a thumb or finger into the mix before thermometers were invented, to determine the proper temperature before adding yeast. The yeast wouldn't grow if the brew was too cold, and if too hot, the yeast would die, thus the phrase "rule of thumb." And beer is generally ordered in pints and quarts in English pubs. Historically in old England, when pub crawlers got unruly, the pub keeper would yell at them to mind their own pints and quarts and settle down, thus the expression "mind your Ps and Qs."

Sure that Dickens had found his way into the Prospect of Whitby, I learned that in the very spot we sat, Dickens had indeed found inspiration for his work. Perhaps he sat at the same window nursing a pint while looking across the Thames at the run-down streets where street urchins ran and where industry carelessly looked upon the small imps as yet another cog in the wheel of progress.

We tipped back many stouts between us before deciding to try some of the pub food. As we finished our dinner, my English counterpart told me that I should try some bread pudding. Whitby's was some of the best he had ever tasted, and he had been eating bread pudding for his entire forty years.

I was so full. Yet I wanted to experience all aspects of the Prospect, so I implored our waitress for a "bread pudding to go." She looked at me dully and said, "Eh?" I said again that I would like to have a bread pudding to go, to which she exclaimed that surely she had no idea what I was talking about. I explained how in the States we always got "to go" when we ate Chinese or pizza. She again asked me to explain how I would want her to go about it, and I realized that in all seven hundred years of the Prospect of Whitby, no one had ever left with a to-go box. I was making history, somehow marking the old Prospect of Whitby uniquely. A strange thought to be sure, but I was on my fourth or so Guinness and ready to make history somehow.

Bread Pudding and Dickens

After understanding what it was I wanted, the waitress returned with the equivalent of a two-foot-by-two-foot piece of Tupperware and holding a lonely little four-inch piece of bread pudding smack dab in the middle with the warm, sweet creamy sauce drizzled about it. After considering that I would be hauling a huge hunk of Tupperware with a relatively miniscule piece of bread pudding back down the hardest streets of London, I reasoned that after such a production, the least I could do was take it to the hotel with me. It was indeed worth the hassle.

Several nights later, still on my quest to cultivate something of Dickens, Andy and I walked in the neighborhood that was reportedly where Dickens had observed the counting houses and the orphans from which he pulled the stories of *A Christmas Carol* and *Oliver Twist*. I stood in amazement as my mind stored the pictures of the buildings, which had stood by the Thames since Dickens. At the entrance of the riverfront streets, more channels than streets, sat another pub. I knew I would never find another pub that held the same amount of mystery and intrigue as the Prospect of Whitby. I had reached the pinnacle of my search and could be done with it … unless, of course … *well, okay, I thought … let's try this one last one then, just in case,* as we nearly passed by yet another charming pub. It might not be where Dickens sat, but for all I knew, maybe this was the pub that inspired the fifty-cent comic character Andy Capp.

★

We Americans soon left London to accomplish our second mission with regret that we were leaving behind the pub culture we had just started to experience. We were to visit our American client's manufacturing facility in the south of France after conducting several important meetings in Paris.

After less than a week in Paris, we were summoned back to London by my client's European senior vice president. Joe and I left our wives to the museums, shops, and wonders of Paris and jumped a plane to cover the short distance back. We were to meet in a small country town outside of London, where the senior vice president of our most important client kept his home. We took a cab to the general vicinity of the office, arriving shortly before supper. Dropping our bags off in our room, we hurriedly asked the hotel clerk for directions to the nearest pub. We would waste no time.

We walked about a quarter mile to a small pub along the side of the road. Inside the quaint country pub, two huge innkeepers met us, creamy white Great Pyrenees with heads the size of giants. The dogs looked us over like a couple of old codgers, wary of our intention, then followed us to our table as though seating us, and then they took up their normal stations near the front door, letting out enormous sighs. When reclined, they looked like a pair of huge polar bear rugs, lifting their heads only upon a sharp sound or someone walking to retrieve darts from his game. The pub had a cozy living room feel, as though it was an extension of someone's house, complete with a crackling fireplace. When a regular patron would enter, the two dogs wagged their enormous tails, following along in a lumbering pace. For a few regulars they would lay at their feet for a short time before returning to their stations by the door.

The menu consisted of six items handwritten on a grease board that apparently changed when the pot ran out. Most of the items we saw on other patrons' plates appeared to be slightly overcooked hunks of meat mixed with greatly overcooked potatoes and other vegetables. But we were there more for the beverage than the food. Getting recommendations from some of the locals, we decided on the same plate of bangers and potatoes, which went well with our beer selections.

We had all but thought our times in the English pubs were over, that it would be some time before we would again experience the pulled Guinness rather than the bottled or tapped stout back home in the United States. We were more delighted about the prospect of having another go at what was now our favorite beverage than even the business at hand. We ordered our usual pub drink, Guinness stout along with some Bass ale, and sampled some of the other regional favorites as we sat deep into the night enjoying this cultural norm.

The prospect of experiencing such a moment would never again be the same. Not since The Prospect of Whitby.

Sandbaggers All

One evening heading into spring some years back, I sat in my office, noticing the diminishing white caps on the Rocky Mountains to the west. The lower foothills were greening, holding the promise of warmer months to come. Winter seemed unusually long that year and my mind was on vacation, sun, and Bermuda.

Several times a year the company I worked for issued contests to inspire excellence, with tangible prizes to be won. That spring, the winning team of each division would be awarded a prestigious trip to Bermuda to rub shoulders with the firm's president and other muckity-mucks at the top of our sales food chain.

The contests were based on hitting certain levels in various categories. Products and services were assigned points. One big order or an accumulation of orders counted toward the end goal. Because of these contests there was a great propensity for sandbagging until the end, leaving everyone in suspense. (*Sandbagging* is a term most often used in poker; it is the practice of holding back information until near the end of a "period" or a hand of cards in order to throw whoever needs to be thrown off the trail.) This technique would dash the hopes of those who just a day before saw their name near the top of the national list, only to have someone in a distant state turn in an order that crushed the rest of the list. Sandbagging was just a part of the game. If one team turned in their numbers too early, it inspired their competitors to try to outdo them. If one team turned in their large contest-winning orders at just the right time, there would be nothing anyone else could do about it—it was just too late. I had some serious competition for the Bermuda contest.

Long after five o'clock the area outside my office was unusually noisy. People were milling around waiting to hear the Bermuda news. My boss walked into my office with a strange smile on his face, holding a piece of paper. He was trying to get my attention. I had no time for his reporting to me of numbers and rankings and quotas, not on this night when all we had worked toward for the Bermuda contest would come to an end, either way.

Earlier in the year my team—consisting of sales, technical services, management, customer service, and support—had been intent on winning the contest for a trip to Bermuda by topping the other winning teams. Excited talk, the coveted Bermuda trip was one of the destinations we dreamed of making. Not only because it meant carefree days on the island while the others of our peers labored away on company time, but because of the sheer ego gratification of winning. It meant once again sending envy up the backsides of our in-office competitive teams that rubbed our faces in their successes repeatedly in the Monday morning meetings before we started hitting our stride.

My team never felt as though we competed with the other office teams, but more so with the teams in distant cities across the country who were in the elite ranks of our specific tasks. If we succeeded in the most unlikely of tasks, we would be the heroes of the entire major accounts sector; if we failed we would be zeros and most likely would be looking for something else to do within the year.

The phantoms we competed against were the crème de la crème of our ranks. There was one woman in particular named Berdetti, who led a team like mine. The company had afforded two teams a position, and I was sure her team would make it along with one other. Before my boss could speak, I asked, "Is Berdetti going?"

The rest of my team except my technical specialist, Joe, jammed into my office, anxiously awaiting his reply.

"Uh, yeah, she is," he replied, his smile diminishing, as if he were up to something that would in the end serve to inspire me but for the short term squash me.

I brushed it off, bolstered myself for the defeat, and assumed that one of my competitors had been sandbagging bigger than my team's sandbag. I squeaked out, "Is Jones's team going?" Knowing if his was, we weren't. Jones was leading a team in Florida, which had been ranked dead last when the first Bermuda rankings hit and had progressively climbed from the bottom to the top. With his team now hovering in the top five, rumors abounded about their commando tactics and their intent to win the contest. Jones had called me several times, and I knew he was calling Berdetti as well to ascertain how we had closed in for the kill. Jones and I had been together in numerous training classes and had some great laughs. We had retired several nights to the hotel piano bar, sipping on porters and stouts and talked about all kinds of things. We had crossed the competitive battle lines and had become friends.

More people crowded into my office followed by the vice president of our division. I spun around in my chair and purposefully eyed the trophies on my shelf from my past successes, hoping to drag her eyes over to them to remember what we had contributed besides our efforts in this contest.

It was time to face the music. I looked pleadingly at my boss to be merciful with the recent arrival of my vice president.

He looked at me and smiled widely. "Nope, Jones isn't going."

My heart lifted. It had been rumored for weeks that the contest was between our three teams, but there was a chance one of the lower teams had surged, though it was highly unlikely. "Did Berdetti top the list?"

"Uh, no ... second place, he said. You guys nailed it! Number one in the country! Congratulations!"

The celebration began at once. I stood and hugged my team. We would revel in our fifteen minutes of fame on the small British island and then for months of limelight like small-town celebrities in our office. Although we all knew it raised the bar of expectation, we were ready to step up to it. We had a few sandbags of our own for the big end-of-year cruise with the president, and now no one would be able to stop or top us.

My lead technical guy, Joe, whom I had spent more time with in the past year than my own wife, walked into the office with his hands full. In one hand he held his favorite rot gut, cheap six-pack of beer, and in the other he held an expensive six-pack of oatmeal stout, which he thoughtfully remembered was one of my favorites. He set the oatmeal stout down on the desk in front of me and reached his right hand across the desk. "We did it!" he beamed. How he had been so sure was a mystery to me.

My nervous boss looked over to our vice president hoping I wasn't going to pop the top off those caps in the office and lose my job right there. She smiled and started to walk out as if to say, "I see nothing." I grabbed the six-packs, and the rest of my office revelers followed in a sort of conga line toward the elevator.

☆

A month later, I sat in a local pub on the seaside road of Bermuda with three members of my team and the other lucky winners. It was a real British-style pub with the same pulled stout system that I had so enjoyed in Britain. I toasted my success with Berdetti after all of the hoopla and hype from the awards the night before. She sipped a pale ale while I enjoyed my stout. We raised a toast to good old Jones who we both thought would have been there. I thought how nice it would be of me to send him a case of microbrews from my home state as a consolation for my time in Bermuda. Still there was his sandbagging potential to consider for the upcoming President's Inner Circle trip. One can never get too chummy.

I looked across the harbor and watched small boats milling in and out of the path of a large cruise ship. I tipped my pint toward the window, then clicked my glass to Berdetti's and said, "To the president's inner circle!" I saw her competitive dander rise. I was planning for the biggest event of the year. She silently calculated what she had to do to be there, too. We were sandbaggers, all.

Echoes of Taos

Some say every man searches for his father his whole life. Sometimes he is found, most often not. I set off to find a bit of my father once in the echoes of the past, without even knowing I was doing so.

Sometimes a homecoming occurs when you're actually pointed in the opposite direction of home. It's a homecoming of sorts if the destination is not a physical place that once was a home but is home to memories of a time that stands out, particularly if that time was pivotal in your life.

As I neared my final destination, Taos, New Mexico, I followed a winding road that wrapped around a beautiful lake. A sudden, hard rain eclipsed the bright, late afternoon sun and set tight down in the valley. Thunder clapped and lightning streaked close by as I inched my way along in the torrential rain on the narrow two-lane road. Signs indicating roadwork ahead slowed the pace of the anemic traffic. Two work crews in huge trucks slowly moved up and down the narrow strip of road.

As I sat in a line of cars in a construction zone, I noticed four men sitting under a tarp, protected from the rain as evening came on. Resting between them were what appeared to be the last of a six-pack of longneck beers. I watched as the men laughed and guffawed and slapped one another's knees in apparent stories of complicity. I wished I could pull over and join them, yet knew I would not be accepted in unless I brought my own six-pack to share and maybe a few stories of my own. I thought of how nice a cold beer would be and wondered how long before I would sit down to a good regional dish with a beer of my own as I waited for the young girl up ahead to flip the sign from STOP to SLOW.

Along the winding canyon road, lights began to blink on in the houses on the hillsides like candle lamps floating down some unseen river. The houses receding into dusk looked much like the houses adorning the sides of mountain roads in my home state of Colorado, except for the reddish adobe clinging to the sides of most. Chile ristras, hung as plentiful as the welcoming wreaths at Christmas, softly blew in the warming summer evening breeze. Ah, New Mexico, the land of enchantment.

★

It had been many years since I had been in Taos. It was a seasonably warm evening after the sudden cloudburst that had held for much of my journey, but now there was no sign of clouds as I approached my destination.

The first stars showed in the still lightened sky as I drove on through the winding, forested hills into Taos. I remember fondly the little sleepy town from my childhood and the times my father would recount the little Plaza in which my brother and I took to dancing in a festival with the Indians. I remember being intrigued with them all: small women crouched in colorful blankets selling turquoise and silver jewelry; warriors in beaded clothing, belled ankles, painted faces, and large, dark eyes. Mostly I remembered the way they captivated a crowd.

I entered the famous Plaza. As I passed several galleries and little shops, I conjured up the times when I walked the same streets with my parents. I resolved to just get to know the little town as it was today and not try to live in the yesteryear memories of our long car trips. My father, on one of our trips to New Mexico, had written a short story set in Taos called "The Festival." I felt my father close and heavy on my mind as I deliberated to find a setting for a story there as well and noted in my journal to dig up his manuscript and reread it. Strangely, I felt as though somehow my father was on this journey with me.

Where I had stayed once as a boy, the Hotel La Fonda de Taos, was now disappointingly surrounded by curios and gift shops. Gone were the Indians dancing. In the lobby I registered for a room and looked around briefly afterward. The sitting area held sparse furniture, painted southwestern hues of blue. Set in a case was a bullfighter's wares, and old hand-carved chairs with bright red leather cushions awaited visitors. Artwork by D. H. Lawrence hung behind an iron bar gate to view for a few dollars. How many times the famous writer must have entered the same lobby. I wondered if my father had been enamored with the idea of D. H. Lawrence drawn to similar inspiration from the Plaza when he came there to write.

I climbed the steps to my room and set my carrying bag on the bed and felt in my pocket for some money. It was time for dinner.

From the street, I imagined my father sitting in the window sketching with words the people who had filled the Plaza with life so many years ago, cultivating the scene and the characters who would soon burn in his brain and in his story. He would have sat there quietly into the dark night, perhaps with a cigarette burning and a can of beer, sipping and composing characters and stories while my mother, my brother, and I slept fitfully in the hot New Mexico night. Imagining myself catching the echoes of my father's thoughts in the Plaza and incorporating them into my own story, I wished my dad had come on this sojourn with me and regretted how little time we spent together anymore. My father was so heavy on my mind. I reasoned it was because the last time I had been in Taos he had been so present with me; somehow he was connected to it all.

I drove down Taos's main road until a large neon sign beckoned me into a restaurant named Fred's, a small cantina. I pulled my car into a dark parking place and went in. The walls were brightly painted orange, the ceiling depicting an angelic sky on one half and eternal fire and damnation on the other. The four walls were adorned with crucifixes of all shapes and sizes: a skeletal Christ made of metal parts, an old Mexican Christ adorned with sunglasses, a crucifix made of broken mirror shards, a crucifix depicting a simple crown of thorns, and a Star of David made of nails. Waitresses adorned with tattooed armbands and various visible body piercings floated about taking orders.

I eagerly ordered blue tortilla chicken enchiladas with green chile and posole and two dark Mexican beers with lime and salt. My waitress, wearing a nose ring, tight turquoise hot pants, and large tattooed armbands at the crease between her biceps and shoulder muscles walked away singing loudly from some opera. Rastafarian music filled the rest of the restaurant and I wondered how she could stay in her operatic lyric with all of the confusion.

My waitress returned with the beers. I sat deep in thought and scribbled notes in my notepad. Just then a very rough-looking man wearing sunglasses walked toward my table staring at me intently. He paused and looked down at me. When he lowered his sunglasses, I saw that his left eye was whitened over. He motioned to the second beer on my table sitting untouched. I looked up at him curiously.

"That for me?" he asked in a low, gravely voice followed by a smirk, almost apologetic as though I might have been expecting him.

A strange tingle ran up my spine. I looked for the manager or at least my waitress.

"You gonna answer me?" He looked at me intently.

"I beg your pardon?"

He just laughed and sat down heavily in the chair opposite of me and looked at the beer again. I noticed a large hunting knife attached to a braided leather belt and holster banging loudly against the table as he settled in across from me.

"I said, is that for me?" All apologies had left his face. His knuckles bore down on the table as he leaned his huge face in toward me, his blank eye staring off. Just then the waitress, still singing, delivered a large basket of blue tortilla chips and some spicy salsa. The scent of cilantro wafted up from the warm bowl and I looked at her pleadingly, but she had already turned from me and was walking to another table.

"Uh ... sure, if you want it," I answered.

By the way he was dressed, I assumed he lived on the streets. He looked to be about ten years my senior and had a long, tightly braided ponytail. I thought maybe if I just gave him the beer he would get up and walk away. I hadn't seen where he came from and didn't know if he had been actually sitting somewhere else in the cantina.

He flipped the lime onto the floor with a dirty middle finger and gulped down about a quarter of the bottle in one swallow. "Mind if I take a few chips?" His manners were fine.

I nodded, wondering if "take" meant that he was leaving.

He swiped a handful, dipped a few in the salsa, and hummed while he ate. "Whatcha writin' about?" He motioned to my notepad. Before I could answer he told me that he liked to write, that once upon a time he had been an English major and had held out big dreams for a career as an author.

He talked about his confusing and life-defining time in Vietnam. I had so often heard that vets don't like to get into the horror and wondered why he was sharing his stories with me. He told me about the wandering he had done since returning to the States, and what a disappointment he was sure he had been to his parents. He talked of a young girl he had loved in high school who had become pregnant while he was away. As though he was telling me stories he had never spoken of before, he mingled his words with memory, anecdotes, and a sort of street-smart wisdom I wouldn't have expected. He called himself simply Jim. I sensed it wasn't really his name, that somewhere along the way he had dumped off his past identity and now lived hand to mouth in the shroud of his memories with his single name.

The waitress came by to tell me that my dinner was coming soon and wondered if I wanted another beer. I eyed mine, which held less than an inch, and Jim's, which was drained sometime before, and nodded for another two.

Jim continued with stories about his past and talked some about his dreams. After draining the last of his second beer, he pushed away from the chair. He looked at me intently, held his hand out, and shook mine and smiled. "Thanks." He walked to the bathroom and then came back out a minute or so later. He nodded acknowledgment to me again and headed out the front door.

I watched him walk down the two-lane road in front of Fred's and considered myself lucky to have met him. For the small price of two beers, he had shared a history with me, he had connected with another human being in passing and was now onto his next stop.

As the waitress placed my dinner on the table and picked up Jim's empty bottles, she saw he had left a quarter under each bottle, his contribution to the tip.

I sat in silence, enjoying my dinner deep in thought about the past few minutes I had spent listening to Jim, thinking of how my father had for years spent time in taverns and bars, sharing stories with others. I remembered evenings, sitting on the stairs of my childhood home, listening to him recount to my mother the colorful characters he had met in Cheyenne or Laramie, Wyoming, at a famous cowboy honkytonk. He would tell my mother how some of the characteristics and idiosyncrasies of the cowboys and cowgirls he had met played right into the people he was writing about in his current novel. In these places he was no longer The Professor or The Associate Dean of Arts, Humanities, and Social Sciences. He was simply a man many years away from the humble farm he had grown up on. He was a man with the right cowboy boots and hat, graced with the speckling of horse manure from his own horse, lending legitimacy to his journey. I thought of the loose, socially ambient attitude I had experienced years before with my dad when we stopped in dark taverns to try to somehow understand each other better. We would do "the guy thing," throwing back longneck bottles while sharing stories and history. My father and I sipped our beer and ate Rocky Mountain oysters across from the old Rialto Theater in the small town just south of my own hometown. He told me stories of his time in Korea during the war, what it was like to grow up in bootleggers' territory in upstate New York, how he had met my mother, and even told me about some of his earlier girlfriends. He shared with me his passion for writing, which I hadn't yet found to be mine. He talked about how each person carried with them many stories and how, if you listened well, you would learn the most extraordinary things from the most ordinary and how by sharing your own stories with others, you could somehow bring back theirs.

Sitting there in Fred's I realized I had fulfilled those same things my father had told me about once. I, too, had come to a point where the writing of stories possessed me and the cultivation of stories from others intrigued me. My father had been a good teacher.

I slipped the key in my door back at the hotel and set a six-pack of beer on the dresser. I relished the thought of sitting out on the tarpaper balcony right outside my room below the windows to write, while sipping on a cold beer on this warm summer night; it would be a fitting tribute to the dream of writing that my father had planted unknowingly in me many years prior.

I stepped out onto the tarred roof with my beer, stretched my legs, and imagined my dad doing the same decades ago. Before I began to write in that place where my dad had so many years earlier, I read his story and understood.

An Occasional Bachelor

I was one of the first in my gang of guys to be smitten, really smitten. When I met her, I knew I was a goner. I was able to picture putting aside my deeper desire to live with the guys, amongst the dirty socks and clothes, loud music, TV dinners, unwashed dishes, and other male cohabitational possibilities to be with her.

I imagine it is true that in certain circles, men gather together to send one of their own into happy matrimony with a glass of wine. But it is the common bachelor party that is possibly the one event inevitably featuring a keg of beer and shots of hard liquor as the main gift for the guest being honored. There is something strangely sadistic about the desire of one's best friends to humiliate and cause the guest of honor to become so inebriated that blackmail could be extorted for the activities that take place during the actual party. A last hurrah for the poor, sorry sap who had just negotiated his own demise for the love of a woman, to which all will raise a glass (or two), and most will succumb to as well in their own good time.

How indignant we all feel when one of our ranks pushes in our face that they would rather spend the majority of their waking hours with one female when they could be out with the guys. Aren't all guys in pursuit of the simple brotherhood of partying and usually looking for the comforts of a woman and then, of course, some getting ensnared and ... hmm? Well, back to the subject of the bachelor party.

Early Twenties Bachelor Party (#1)

I would have not just one bachelor party, but two. My best man, Michael, hosted the first and was the one for whom I'd wait too many years to pay back his hospitality. We started in a normal, partying fashion; one by one the friends joined, none on time, of course, but all bearing wonderfully creative bachelor party gag gifts. The keg ordered by my best friend and fellow beer lover was not the normal bachelor party fare; it was a rich lager, generally one to be savored not chugged. A good idea until the idea totally lost its value as we started in on the first of the night's drinking games. The party switched to high gear, twenty-some-odd guys involved in chugging contests, several more intent on winning than others.

As things progressed it was decided that we move the party to a local tavern where I had worked for three years, putting myself through college on tips and $2.01 an hour. I had quit my job the week prior, but my previous fellow workers and friends from the tavern were interested in pitching in for the celebration. The equivalent of about a fifth of Jack Daniels in shots, along with beer chasers, was lined up in front of me, and one by one I downed them, endeavoring not to disappoint my party-going mates.

At one point during the party, the guys lined up and down the sides of a long table, and some began chanting

"Speech, speech" as though somehow I could make sense to them why a man in his early twenties would embark on matrimony. I began to bang a beer bottle on the tabletop to get everyone's attention (some of this has been related to me after the fact, for some of my own recollection is mercifully a little cloudy). As soon as all eyes were upon me, I said, "I am going to throw up," which I proceeded to do under the table, between my knees, and some of my buddies' shoes. There was the answer they all sought to the mystery of it all. The men went back to reveling in their own bachelorhood. A short time later I was standing (actually being held up) in the bathroom by my best man's brother and my fiancée's cousin, graciously giving their shoes in sacrifice to my bachelor party as I missed the porcelain.

Later, several of my friends kindly took me to my parents' house to remove my contact lenses so I wouldn't awaken the next morning feeling as though two stones had been gouging at my eyelids all night from the inside. I moved from the bathroom counter in my attempt to replicate the habit of contact removal to the toilet to relieve myself further of the massive quantities of beer I had drunk earlier and the remaining Jack Daniels comingling, to bring an otherwise never seen hue of green to my skin. My mother mercifully held my head as I would heave yet another time.

How many times had my mother seen me in the perils of sickness? How many times had she nursed me back to health in her loving way that only a mother can? This time, though, it was slightly different. She, too, would laugh at me the way the bachelors did when I said something that was left completely up to interpretation.

Gently, my mother held my head over the hole of the toilet, mostly from fear of my baptizing the entire bathroom with bachelor party reverie (though she found the antics of the boys amusing and was relieved that in my condition we had someone "smart" enough to designate himself as the safe driver). I am sure she must have wondered what that sweet young girl she had come to think of as her own daughter already was getting herself into with me.

When we returned to the party, most of the guys went back to sipping beers and watching some selected movies, all the while I spent time very close to a trash can in lieu of sleeping in the bathroom.

The next morning I awoke with the largest head I'd ever had, pounding with pain no bottle of aspirin could stop. We were crashed in several rooms, and the stale smell of beer and pizza met my nose, threatening me to once again bob in the trash can. Strewn about on the coffee table of my friend's parents' house were Polaroids of me and several of my other unfortunate bachelor party pals in hilarious (only hilarious now) poses. The distinct hue of green was all mine. My cousin, a hard-partying Texan, fashioned a full-faced hat out of a twelve-pack carton of beer and danced around me in some ritualistic dance as I left off consciousness for a short while. Many of the stories of that night would have to be relayed to me secondhand—that is, when I could actually lift my head on my own.

Early Twenties Bachelor Party (# 2)

A week later, the night before I was to be married, we all met again for round two of bachelor party reverie. This time we rented a hotel room. This time I sat back and observed most of the drinking games, carefully sipping on just a couple of beers rather than joining in as actively as before. This time I used my head.

More incriminating pictures were taken of several of my buds who had one too many gin and tonics and one too many bottles of beer that were used as darts for the bull's-eye we drew on the hotel wall with a lipstick found in the parking lot. We had some fun with the lipstick after several of the groomsmen passed out. Their photographs would be the amusement the next morning. This time I was taking the photographs.

Many more stories came from that night, but unfortunately I have been sworn to secrecy. Just use your imagination and be sure to include some very large female undergarments and lots of blackmail potential.

Early Thirties Bachelor Party

I lay in waiting for many years for my best man, Michael, to succumb to a certain woman's wiles. It took a decade of plotting and patience, but I would indeed have my retribution. Along with another of his good friends, I arranged a wonderful, "mature man's" bachelor party to match more of our "sophisticated, now grown-up" interests. We rented out a private room at the famous Wyncoop Brewery in lower downtown Denver for a gathering of men to send off one of the last bachelors to matrimony. We thoughtfully arranged to have his brothers and father present and ensured him I harbored no evil feelings in what was only a distant memory—a time of learning, a long-forgotten mistake we had made in our youth. Yet for the weeks preceding the party, he questioned me over and over regarding my vow once to pay him back someday.

This was to be a regular, mature man's party with a sit-down dinner, a large array of wonderful beers, first brought out on tasters' platters to be sipped and enjoyed, none of the old kegger foolishness for this gathering. We had all grown up and were maturely approaching the seriousness of the bonds of matrimony with a much cooler head than we had in the past.

The evening proceeded as planned: For every beer ordered around, Michael got two, and of course the obligatory shots. Subtly, oh so subtly, we slipped him into complacency, until hours later he found himself stripped and strapped down inside a shower in just his boxer shorts with a pretty and buxom young lady spraying him with whipped cream. Several hours later, I mercifully held his head in my hand as he threw up our hard-spent money onto the driveway of an all-night diner. Ah, revenge can be so sweet.

I tried to muster sympathy, but empathy was still too close, and retribution does have its good points. After all, this was the guy who painted all of my toenails bright fuchsia during another lapse of sobriety and judgment on my part the night of my twenty-first birthday. He surely had it coming.

The wonder of guys is that we still speak to each other with no regrets and no further grudges; all is even. Michael and I currently have lunch together on a regular basis, but since that night he has never ordered more than two beers when we go to a ball game or out to dinner. Some of us seem to learn faster than others.

Mid—thirties Bachelor Party

Recently I attended a bachelor party for my brother-in-law in California. He was one of the last holdouts to matrimony, waiting until he reached his midthirties and felt he had the right stuff to offer and the time was right for commitment. His party was held in a tavern with a live band and was a good mix of men, older and younger, all reveling in the celebration. This round we were indeed much more mature and had lost the desire to embarrass or humiliate the guest of honor. No one was intent on getting the groom drunk, with the exception of one of my sister-in-law-to-be's cousin, who seemed to take his drinking very seriously and was downing three for each one the rest of us had downed from the start. He didn't meet a drink he didn't like, no matter what someone was ordering; he would order one, too.

When I was young we would mix Dr. Pepper, orange soda, Coca-Cola, and 7-Up and call it a Suicide. I tried to imagine an apt name for mixing whisky, beer, wine, gin, and many other drinks—the only name coming to mind immediately was a Major-Suicide-Hangover. Those of us who had come from Colorado and have known one another for years, but see each other infrequently, sipped on porters and stouts and remarked on our recent successes and failures.

Overall, this was the most civil bachelor party I had ever attended. (There is indeed something to be said for waiting until you are mature enough to handle yourself.) The first phase of the party adjourned the small jazz tavern to a racier nightclub in the tony part of Santa Monica, California. I noticed the father of the groom and the father of the bride gracefully exiting, and thoughts of bachelor parties gone badly in my past came flooding to memory. We overheard a gentleman at the table next to ours bragging on a project he was working on with Arnold Schwartzenegger. He had the looks, the build, and the fat wallet to convince the small throng of women around him that he was the real deal. When one of the groomsmen made mention to the band playing that we had a bachelor on a short leash in the crowd, the Schwartzenegger body double, apparently not wanting anyone to one-up him, offered a round to those of us hanging with the soon groom-to-be.

A round of shots was delivered to the table. One of the groomsmen in attendance and I were having a nice conversation about our children and weren't excited about "shooting

Jell-O shots" at this juncture of the evening. We politely accepted, raised our glasses to the host of the rounds, then to the
groom, pretended to down them, and then set them back on
the table, laughing and returning to our conversation.

The aforementioned bride's cousin, who now had
quite a head on, made his way around the table. He finished
not only the unshot shots but also drained the rest of the glasses of whatever was left on the table as the party began to
adjourn and we all set out to head back home. With several
miles to walk, a couple of us took it upon ourselves to "baby-
sit" the cousin, to assure he made it back to the hotel alive. He
spoke to light poles, trees, and every other object along the
road. He wrapped his arms around each of the guys one by
one, exclaiming how we were all family now and sloppily
extolled his affection for us one and all. Several of us secretly
devised a plan to tie him to a street lamp and let him sleep it
off vertically. We thought better of leaving him on a busy
California street, and eventually escorted him to his room,
wondering what his wife would do when she saw his condition.
With the exception of the actual wedding ceremony, which
mercifully for him was not until the next evening, we saw nothing more of the cousin.

I prefer now to sit around with my friends quietly
over a beer or two. No longer are the beer bongs, kegger parties, or chugging contests a part of our common goal. More
often than not, we simply find a small pub or microbrewery
with character, and talk about times past, issues present, and
plans for the future. Usually we are all home in time to tuck
our young ones in.

But wait, what is this? An invitation to another bachelor
party at one of *those* places … hmmm, this could be fun … now
let me remember, what did he do to me at *my* bachelor party?

Men's Night Out

Everyone has to have a hobby. When I first took on the hobby of brewing my own beer, I milled through an old-fashioned, small, dusty brew shop while a tough-looking young man watched me from one of those bulbous mirrors hanging in the corner, allowing him to observe the entire store. The mirror was the only modern addition in the converted old house. I was there with a friend, one much more knowledge-able in "brew speak" than me. I felt as though I was in a for-eign land as the two discussed chocolate malts, specialty hops, carboys, ambient temperatures, and other terms in the com-mon vernacular of the homebrew group. The archaic feel of the shop, as well as what felt like the good old way of doing things, enticed me to become a part of brewing as a hobby.

The thought of making my own brew was much the same as the gratification I get from raising vegetables in my garden. Somehow they always taste better when planted by your hand than those purchased at the store. I reasoned that brewing beer must be much the same.

My first batch would be an IPA, an India pale ale. As I read the ingredients on the labels of some of the premade mixes, the thought of brewing a fruit beer for the holidays intrigued me. I had my own fruit trees. I started to imagine the blending of my gardening desires with my desire to drink fine beer. I imagined warm summer nights spent weeding or cultivating in the coolness of the garden with a pint of my own homebrew. Up until this point there were only two real associations beer had to my gardening: the pints I would take out to my plot as I weeded, harvested, and planted, often wandering from the garden to the barbecue grill on summer evenings; and the ounces I would lay out in trays overnight in which to beckon the nasty slugs. The theory of beer and slugs is that slugs love beer. The slug smells the beer, crawls into the shallow bowl, becomes drunk, and cannot climb back out, therefore drowning in its libation (a distant reminder to bachelor parties past comes to mind). I thought of submitting a humorous essay regarding beer and gardens titled "Beer Gardens—Where the Gardeners 'Slug' It Out" to either *Zymurgy* magazine or to one of the horticulture magazines I subscribe to and realized it was time to stop working so hard.

I examined the various cans of beer mix while my friend chose loose grains to grind and fresh hops. He smiled the look of a seasoned vet at me, the rookie, and assured me that it wouldn't be long before I was engrossed in the hobby as he was. I watched his two bags fill with ingredients and new equipment. I picked out the makings needed for a rookie brewer, including an IPA mix and a wheat beer mix to which I had plans of adding my own tree's apples for the Christmas brew, a Granny Smith wheat beer. The glass carboys were the same as the two sitting at home collecting my loose change, so I reasoned I was well on my way to becoming a master brewer.

Across the city were four other men doing the same thing, preparing for our "guy's night" where we would gather and learn from the real masters. We were to meet at one friend's house later that evening to combine the expertise of my accomplice in the store, all of us with the desire to learn more.

That night we learned how to grind the grains, boil the wort, strain the wort, balance the sugars, how to properly store the finished batch, and all of the other particulars we would need to know when we brewed in our own kitchens the next night. We sipped from previous brews our friend had made and marveled how the ale fashioned after the recipe of Bass ale tasted remarkably similar—no, better, most of us responded in compliment to our teacher—hoping his generosity wouldn't abate.

We went on a tour of his basement, where he kept cases of his beer chronicled, labeled, and rotated. Indeed he was a man who took his beer seriously. We each selected a bottle from his cache. I sipped an oatmeal stout. Those of us with a penchant for the dark stuff marveled at how our teacher had captured the taste we all longed to strive to create.

Envy, a sense of competition, rose within me. I wanted to brew such a tasty and handcrafted beer. The excitement welled as we each imagined our first batches of homebrewed beer. I imagined my IPA rivaling the Samuel Smith IPA I enjoy on special occasions. I imagined my Granny Smith wheat beer winning awards and compliments from my buddies. I envisioned a label I could fashion for my own handcrafted beer and that I would become so proficient at the craft that I would soon be assembling handcrafted sampler six-packs that would be this year's holiday take-along to the parties we would attend. Soon I would parlay my natural talents into the running of a wildly successful microbrew pub. I figured I could brew two cases every weekend and store up enough beer to give as holiday presents and to age in my basement for those special occasions, all carefully labeled, dated, and cataloged like my friend's. I would soon learn that our thoughtful host had saved us all from the labor of an integral and mostly monotonous aspect of beer brewing: the sterilization process, which would nip in the bud some of my excitement for brewing beer every weekend.

The evening was going along very well. It was fun to sample the beers that we could each be on the brink of creating. We all worked together to bring forth another batch, handcrafted from the start with homegrown hops, hand-ground grains, secret tips, and more lore on the history of beer brewing than one could read in a book. All the while, men who I had known only professionally were revealing themselves. Somehow in our complicit bonding, we were finding a way to open up. I have long thought that most men require a prop to communicate well. Usually a man requires a pint in hand before he will reveal much of the inner workings. Something about vulnerability at play that a simple beer diffuses. Relative strangers started to share their stories, their pasts, dreams, and desires.

As the evening wore down, the carboys were filled. We all started to depart one by one, with the assurances from the two master brewers that they were only a phone call away. When I got home I pulled out my new homebrew book in preparation to make my first batch and now excited to get started contemplating taking the next day off from work to do so.

I worked on my first batch with much excitement. After my batch stopped boiling and reached the right specific gravity, it was ready to be sifted into the carboy. I was now just weeks away from savoring my first batch. Though the only real deviation to the canned recipe was my special selection of yeast and extra hops that my knowledgeable friend had recommended, it was still my own brewed batch, made by my own hands. As I got better at it, my beer brewing would soon take on its own personality, too.

I started reading about all kinds of things one could do to make one's beer special and imprint it the way the microbrewers do. I read about a prize-winning batch including new growth from a spruce tree and others including home-grown chilis added into the mix, and I reasoned that I would soon create an assortment of beers to which my garden could contribute, quickly ruling out broccoli and beets.

For a week the carboy churned and roiled. Checking on it often, I measured the specific gravity daily and sipped from the beer extracted, marveling at the premature taste and offering a taste to anyone within the vicinity. Finally the evening came when I knew it was ready. I would bottle my beer the next morning. I pulled out my capper, my caps, and all of the other things I needed for my brew. As I assembled all of my ingredients, I realized I had forgotten the all-important sugar. There was no way I could bottle my beer without brewing sugar. I rummaged through the pantry. I came upon some cane sugar and wondered if I could use it. I called one of the "experts" I had learned from and his response was "Sure, why not? You said you wanted it to have your special signature." I wondered if he was being condescending and if I would ruin my batch, but he assured me it would work fine.

I went to the basement to haul the bottles I had been saving up to the kitchen so I would be ready for the dreaded sanitation process.

Meanwhile, one of my pals looked for a place to store his carboy of dark amber liquid unbeknownst to his wife, and he set the full carboy in the dark clothes closet in their bedroom, anticipating with great joy the magic that would occur there. One afternoon as his beer was coming closer to bottling, his phone rang; when he answered it, it was his wife—furious. Back home in the security of the darkness of their clothes closet, his amber brew had exploded all over her clothing. When he recounted this story to me later, I asked him if he weren't still going to bottle what was left in his carboy. He flashed me an indiscernible look.

Others were reporting a strange taste when they sipped the extracted beer for specific gravity testing. One said that his had an almost medicinal taste. One complained of too much bitter (we would find out that he had boiled his hops bag for the entire boil, instead of the five-minute finishing recommended). Only two of us were still convinced we were sitting on what could easily be mistaken as professionally brewed microbrew; the rest would serve as slug bait.

☆

Several weeks later I pulled the first bottle from its case and poured the contents into a glass, marveling at just the right amount of head. The body of the beer seemed stable, the color against the light a wonderful amber gold. I felt proud as I pulled it to my lips and sipped from the very first real beer made at my own hands. It didn't taste much like my favorite Samuel Smith's IPA, but it didn't taste bad. I was hooked. In spite of the laborious and painstaking sanitizing, I would indeed make many more batches of homebrewed beer. Now that I had my carboy free and another to spare I thought maybe

I would endeavor to make my Granny Smith wheat beer, and I would venture back down to my local brew shop and start contemplating my own grinder.

I packed a six-pack of my IPA into my car and headed to my teacher/friend's house again. We were all to meet there with a six-pack of our own industry to share and get comments on. Our friend who had blown up his first batch showed with a six-pack of some professional microbrew that he had poured into plain bottles and recapped, passing it off as his own. We all got a kick out of that. The others showed with their own batches, and we compared, shared stories, shared knowledge, and in general had a great time.

★

I thought of another time with the same group of friends. Our host, a serious brewer, had told me on numerous occasions about the hops he had grown on the side of his house for his special batches of beer. A new respect for him had grown as I realized the seriousness and the gravity of his occupation with the perfect homebrew. I leafed through the library of homebrew books in his den and noticed that they were all dog-eared and beer splattered from previous experiments and experiences. As a growing group of men gathered in our host's kitchen, his wife and children absent from the home, we began to imbibe in a past batch of smooth lager made at the hand of this master brewer. I began to grind some grains for the batch we were brewing, and again the many stories began to come forth. The more homebrew that poured, the more colorful and stretched the stories became. We all laughed and grimaced. As we gathered around the beverage of choice, we bonded, we shared stories, we did the guy thing again.

I felt a sense of envy as I realized my friend had created more of an art with his homebrew than my simple pre-ground grain, stovetop boiled, brew-shop supplied, carboy-curing, beer-batching mixes. The snow covered the ground thickly as we continued into the night.

Later, we all sat in the living room sipping beer, talking about our frustrations at work, of upcoming vacations, and we even dipped briefly into the tumultuous waters of our relationships with our wives. One of the guys there had recently gotten married, so the rest of the pack felt the need to help him along. At times I found myself nearly rolling on the ground listening in on some of the hilarious mistakes and miscalculations each of us had made.

Over an evening of beer and beer brewing new and deeper friendships were forming, defenses lowering, allowing for that mysterious male bonding that would prove to pay off in the years to come. After all, everyone needs a hobby.

Granddad

One sunny yet cool fall day in the Rocky Mountains, I spent the afternoon talking to my Grandfather about his early days. He spoke tenderly of his times with Grandmother when they were young. He talked of how the world once had been and how, in many ways, he wished it could be so again. He told me of the days as a farm boy in Kansas during Prohibition when he and his five brothers would return from the fields for a midday supper. I explained I was writing a book about the travels, travails, and moments of independence and that I was curious about some of *his* travels.

How many stories he could share after spending nine decades on this earth; how much he had seen! He told me about the beers that he and one of his brothers, Buddy, would boil while Prohibition attempted to keep them from imbibing.

"The government regulated what we were and weren't to drink," he said. "The common thought of the day was that Kansas voted dry and drank wet. My brother would toss in some potatoes to the malt and up went the stuff!" Grandfather chuckled and then smiled wryly, apparently lost in a place where I couldn't join him as though he were physically back in the small kitchen of his youth, making homebrew with Buddy again. "I've always been a hops man. If you can taste the hops, then you can taste the beer. Hops is what makes the beer. I have never liked the watered-down beer they make nowadays."

I told Grandfather about some of my favorite hoppy beers that the local microbreweries served and bottled. He smiled and suggested that maybe I should bring some of that "good stuff" around one day for a few games of shooters (billiards) and drinks.

We talked more about his earlier years; he had spent much of his life "working on the railroad." He reminisced about the days in the old roundhouse. When the men would gather about and slug from the mug and play cards, while hobos slyly jumped onto boxcars heading out of Denver, thinking they hadn't been seen, when in reality the men in charge simply didn't want to jeopardize the fellowship that had been created. Men in his day had a much rougher way of showing any sort of affection, and men in the railroad business were often even rougher than most.

"Salt of the earth, those guys. Any one of them would give you the shirt off their back or help your family out when you needed it. Do people your age still do that?" The question seemed rhetorical.

I had seen so many black and white photographs of Grandfather from his days now past, when he wore fedoras, always looking well dressed and ready to go to his next social event. No matter the occasion, back then the men wore ties and sports coats, looking better dressed on a casual Saturday drive than most modern men look on their most dressed-up days. The photographs of him were generally taken next to a motorcar as though he was constantly either arriving or departing.

Grandfather had grown up in a world that to him has since gone crazy. He talked about the politicos of today and the issues that my sons were confronting in this world and how things were spinning out of control. That if he had as a young man even mentioned the things that are now commonplace, he would have been put in the loony bin. As he nostalgically spoke again of himself and Buddy bottling and capping the beer in the days of Prohibition, he thought those were the days to cherish and look back to for some direction.

"Life was harder in many ways then, but more made sense," he said.

I wondered about inviting Grandfather over to brew some of our own hoppy stuff and to hear more of his stories and get his special potato recipe.

We spent the rest of the cool autumn afternoon hiking in the forest, me listening to his stories and taking mental notes, gleaning wisdom from one who had spent enough years accumulating it. Grandpa spun story after story about the old days, as though most of the good living took place before now. I thought of how someday I would talk to my own grandchildren about my past and realized I was living my good old days right now.

☆

Several weeks later, I showed up at Grandpa's apartment with a six-pack of hoppy beer. We headed to the common room of the retired living complex where the pool table was set. As we entered the room, three gray-haired men who eyed the six-pack under my arm greeted us with cheerful hellos and asked Grandpa, "So, who is this young man?"

Grandpa proudly introduced me. Beers were passed around and then the stories began to flow as we racked up the pool balls and chalked our cues. I had no reason to say much, as I listened to the men's exchange and realized that the rough-and-tumble way they talked to each other was much the same as with me and my buddies. The afternoon passed slower and more relaxed than I am used to, but I thought it was something I would like to do again soon. But the next time I go, I think I better take a twelve-pack; by now, word has probably gotten around about Grandpa's grandson and all the side bets he lost to the pool-playing foursome.

Daredevils

Many guys have a friend who lives on the edge, someone willing to go places no one else treads. Usually it is that one friend who hasn't tied the knot of matrimony or hasn't had the kids yet who most challenge the more domestically inclined of us. The one who chides you about being "whipped," not wearing the pants in the family just because on the drop of a dime you won't jump on a Harley with a sleeping bag and take off for a cross-country cruise or go to the local tattoo parlor after a few too many brewskies for a small, discreet tattoo on your ankle.

He is the friend who likens the potential for a week away with a pal to be like Peter Fonda and Jack Nicholson in *Easy Rider*—free to let the wind blow in his hair, free from encumbrances, and on and on he explains as you nod blankly and wonder if tonight is trash and recycle night and if you need to rotate the tires on your wife's minivan. As he talks about the sexy young lady who has taken a fancy to him at the office, your mind drifts off again, wondering if you missed your turn to shuttle the kids and their friends to soccer practice, and did you remember the promise you made to go over math facts with your child? You suddenly surmise that maybe it would have been a good idea to call home from the office before meeting for a few cold ones to make sure you had a handle on the chores you were scheduled to do.

Ah, domestic bliss. He is the one who gives you grief because at six o'clock on a Friday night you are not willing to tell your wife that you are going out with the guys and "take a stand like a man" and say, "No, I don't know when I will be home dammit!" as she stands in the kitchen finishing cooking dinner while your kids whine at her feet.

One of my childhood pals is one of those guys. Mark was a committed bachelor for many of the years that I've been married. He is an adventurer, the kind of guy you read about in *Outside* magazine (that is, he was until he became husband and father to two young boys, both at this writing still in diapers). He has taught me to spelunk in caves, to hike and climb down off sheer mountain cliffs, to rock climb, to ride places on my mountain bike no man was intended to go, to camp under the stars, and find sustenance from the land around us. We have hiked an extra ten miles to get to a special natural lean-to in the mountains he knows about to save the weight of a tent. We have spent days together in the backcountry, nary seeing more than a few other humans in all the time we've hiked, camped, and lived off the land.

He has chided me about the weight I allow in my backpack when we endeavor to camp deep into the twisting mountain, sometimes foraging our own paths. The odd paradox is that he has never protested the fact that as we have saved an ounce here and a pound there with his high-tech equipment, we meanwhile packed in a six-pack of microbrewed beer.

One time on a camping trip, we set out from our cars with a cooler that we held between us, then took turns hoisting it alone when the path got too twisty and narrow. All of that extra work would give us a few hours of solitude when we would spread our sleeping bags out around a campfire and sip from the icy beer so far away from civilization that sometimes we made up childish imagination games like we had as boys. We would fancy ourselves as explorers, hiking into unchartered territory, seeing things we imagined for the first time, then someone else's garbage would jar us back into reality.

It was those nights when we would talk about the future, what it would hold, long before either one of us had a career, wives, children, or anything else that made our fantasy time in the mountains just that, a fantasy. The crackling fire and the stars hanging over our heads in the inky sky provided true male bonding. I understood then why some people escape society and ferret themselves away in a small cabin in the woods getting lost to all of the rest of the world.

Two guys just hanging next to a campfire, sipping beer, and grilling their dinners on sticks; it just doesn't get any better than that.

★

Right outside of the hometown that my adventure buddy Mark and I grew up in is a canyon stretching a long way between Colorado and Wyoming. The road twists and turns along a river that is reputed to hold some of the best fishing around. We both cut classes all day Friday while in college, leaving early for our adventure and planning to return sometime Sunday. We left our car in a small parking lot designated for hikers and campers and set off for a guy's weekend in the wild. We hiked most of the morning far away from the civilized world, following a map Mark had marked up the last time he was up there to remind himself where the best spots were.

We set up our camp on the eastern face of a tall mountain so the sun would awaken us with the orange blur up there on top of the world. We then endeavored to hike to the very top of the western side of the same mountain ridge, where the sunset view promised to be spectacular. On our backs, we carried a daypack with provisions for a well-deserved mid-evening snack.

As I climbed over a large rock outcropping at the crest of the hill, I was seeing something straight out of *Exodus*; we had climbed so high we had apparently climbed onto holy ground. God was going to meet us right where we were. A huge rock burned bright orange in front of me, moving like fire. Was I in fact seeing a vision or under the intoxicating influence of oxygen deprivation? We hadn't imbibed yet, but still in front of me was an undeniable burning rock. I stuttered Mark's name and urgently told him to get up there with me. He came over the ledge and stood staring at what I was pointing at. In front of us a rock angrily boiled with reddish-orange fire. The late evening orange clouds painting the sky above us added to the intensity of the moving color. I looked to my hiking boots and wondered if we would soon be commanded to take our shoes off and approach, imagining my hair instantly turning white like Charlton Heston's *Moses*.

Mark, a seasoned hiker and camper, said, "This is a first. I've heard about this but haven't seen it firsthand." He walked to the rock, and sliding his hand along its face scooped up a handful of ladybug beetles. A huge mountain hatch of ladybugs was moving across the boulder.

We reclined on the edge of the cliff, boulders at our back propping us up as though we were sitting in a living room watching television. Mark propped his daypack onto his lap and pulled out two bottles of beer, some string cheese, and a pack of salty crackers. We dove in greedily. We watched the sun setting behind a range of mountains to the west of us and looked across the incredible expanse of Colorado's Rocky Mountains all the way into Wyoming.

The next day we tied a rope off on one of the towering pine trees on the same cliff. I had noticed the ladybug beetles were absent as we climbed to our mark. We repelled, descending the expanse of the cliff, and then hiked back up to the top. We roped off on several other places and when the sun had risen high in the sky my stomach began to churn. We hiked back down to our hovel where our foodstuff was stored and pulled out a simple makeshift lunch. He offered a dark beer to me and said. "Hey, it's five o'clock somewhere!" We were done climbing for the day.

☆

My daredevil pal has since mellowed with age and responsibility. With spring coming, we recently talked about a fishing and camping trip with our boys. While we were on the phone, I heard him telling his son that we were all going to go camping. Though he tried to cup the receiver, I overheard him say, "And no diapers in the tent. Big boys go out in the woods," as he attempted the bribe to potty-train.

The strangest things tame some daredevils; domesticity took him down eventually as it had all of us. As we planned for the upcoming camping trip, one with four boys in tow, I checked off "good microbrew" under the list of foodstuff. This time like the others, although we would be packing in a six-pack or two, on this camping trip we'd also be packing in a six-pack of root beer and would be camping considerably closer to the truck, where a sixty-four pack of diapers were.

It's funny how life works. Mark sold his Harley to spend more time on domestic chores. Meanwhile, my boys have grown up to the point that they usually have more plans with their friends than me, freeing me up to do all those daredevil activities. Now I camp more while my whipped friend considers a trip to McDonalds' Playland with two busy boys exhausting and thinks that by taking the screens off a hotel window, it counts as camping. They say daredevils are hard to tame. He'll be back …

A Better Workbench

Women have more sophisticated taste as a rule than men. Where men settle for simplicity, women seem to appreciate the deeper things in life. Women can pull deeper meaning out of common experiences that most men give a "Tool-Time Tim" grunt to and will go on as if nothing of import has happened. Women appreciate the sophisticated nuance of, say, a good wine, a good book, a good conversation, having the ability to multitask. Whereas the common, everyday man finds as much relevance in a good set of crescent wrenches, an ice cold beer with a cheap-o sports team coolie insulating it, and a good thick paste wax for a warm Sunday afternoon job of buffing out the overly equipped four-by-four. All the while, with a beer in one hand, a good sports talk show on the A.M., and a chamois, a man has just a little slice of heaven. Toss in a pleasant, no-issue conversation with a friendly neighbor about cars, bars, or a better workbench arrangement and the day seems complete. All is well with the world.

I have even heard from numerous female sources (and yes of course to every "rule" there is always the exception) that beer is mostly a man's drink. Moreover, men seem often to see beer as one, if not two, of the four basic food groups. That men cannot hold an intelligent conversation unless beer is deemed the conduit for the gathering seems to be conventional thinking. Wine is the more likely the female beverage of choice. Like the Mars and Venus analogies, there simply are no good ways to explain the indescribable differences between the sexes—and when it comes down to it, there's no real reason to try.

All in all, one of the baser pleasures is beer. Though it comes in all flavors, degrees of color, composition, bitterness, and taste, the essential aspect of beer is that it quenches a thirst like no other beverage. Imagine for a moment your favorite pepperoni pizza with a glass of milk rather than a beer. Imagine a bratwurst with mustard and sauerkraut at the ballpark with an icy cold glass of lemonade rather than a cold beer. Though these other beverages may suffice, there is no comparison really, is there? Imagine a group of guys bonding over a poker party with cigars and Kool-Aid rather than an accumulation of beer bottles. Beer is simply an essential ingredient for guys and many of the things guys gather to do together.

★

Recently, my sister-in-law came to my house and observed a large carboy of homebrew curing under my wife's kitchen desk (of course it was there to my wife's dismay that I had forgotten to carry it to the basement before the company showed).

My sister-in-law said, "What is it about men and their compulsion to brew beer?"

I looked at her dully, resentfully, and defensively.

She continued. "My grandfather brewed beer, my uncle brewed beer, my father brews beer, my husband brews beer, and here I find my brother-in-law brews beer, too?! Just what is it with you guys?" She looked over to my wife and my other sister-in-law in a complicit way. They all just rolled their eyes as if to say, "We've all been here before; get used to it. It is just what guys do—no reason to overanalyze it."

I didn't have the heart to tell her that it was me who first got her new husband into brewing beer long before she happened to come into his life. That he and I have shared recipes, ideas, and enthusiastically have discussed the day-to-day changes our particular batches have undergone the way a child's life is charted and followed by a new mother. How could she know that, over the years, her new husband and I had shared many a long-distance conversation, speaking to the various brews we had cooking or curing? How could she know that we had made pacts to brew special beers for the holidays, in a traditional beer swap, like she and my wife perhaps would with baked cookies? That her husband had packed bottles of his own homebrew into his carry-on luggage to bring home to share with me seemed now to be a thing of the past. Ah, another one bites the dust. But soon enough, after the marital passions subside a little and he moves back to his old ways, maybe we will once again share our hobby, when the "honeymoon is over" and she meets the real him, heh heh.

Furthermore, I couldn't have told her at that moment that beer and beer brewing were the only common ground of conversation that I had found with some of her own relations the night of her wedding to my brother-in-law. One of her male relations and I swapped recipes for our favorite lagers and wheat beers, and it was I who introduced him to a new way of using all of those extra apples from his apple trees.

These discussions of beer brewing occurred on the very night that she danced into her own marital bliss.

In ancient Babylon, for the month after a wedding, the bride's father would supply his son-in-law with all the mead he could drink. Although technically mead is a honey wine, the concept of brewing one's own for an elevated effect applies. Because the Babylonians' calendar was lunar based, this period was called the "honey month" or what we know today as the "honeymoon." One wonders just what the expectation of the first month of marriage to the daughter of such father-in-laws was that they assumed the need to intoxicate his new son-in-law for an entire month after making his vows. There must have been some real cases of PMS (post marital syndrome) the father-in-law was trying to buffer. The way my sister-in-law grumbled about the beermaking habits of the men in her life, I thought we should both, her father and myself, pitch in a good quantity of beer to keep my brother-in-law in beer for a month to buffer the days to come.

Back in the kitchen, my sister-in-law continued to comment on the strong intrigue with beer and brewing among much of the menfolk. I just looked at her with my dull knowing smile and said, "Hmmm, guess it's just a guy thing. Stupid, huh?" and gave my most conjured-up simpleton look.

She had donned an apron and joined my wife and other sister-in law in the traditional holiday baking. She continued rolling out the dough for another batch of cookies, threw another knowing glance in the direction of the other women in the room, and dismissed me summarily. With that I noisily grabbed a cold bottle of beer and joined the other men in the family room to watch a football game.

My little niece, Cee Cee, who is just a pint-sized little thing, came running in to the living room, took one look at the television, and rolled her eyes at "that stupid game," which all the menfolk sat gaping at.

Oh boy, I thought. *We'll have to keep her out of the kitchen before she turns on us completely.*

She jumped up into my lap and began to peel the label on my bottle of beer and whispered in my ear, "Uncle Justin, did you know there is a big present under your Christmas tree for me?"

I looked into her big blue eyes, eyes that always melt this uncle's heart and said, "Yeah, who do you think put it under there?"

She looked at me and said, "You? What is it?"

I nodded and shook my head, indicating that she wasn't going to pry the secret out of me and then gazed back at the television. She hugged my neck tightly, excited about the prospect of what lay under the tree, and then looked at the bottle of beer in my hand and said, "Uncle Justin, can I have a sip of your beer?"

I looked at her mischievous face and said, "Sure ... when you are old enough," kissed her on the cheek, and gave her a squeeze.

She wrinkled up her brow in her most disgusted look at my response, curled her little body into my chest and said, "But Uncle Justin, I juuuust looooove the taste of beeeeeer."

Maybe all this "beer is for guys" talk is just that, just talk. I plan to be there when my little niece turns twenty-one. I will buy her first legal beer. That is, if it is still cool to hang out with the old guy. Then we will slip down to the local homebrew store and I will teach her the trade and tradition that has been handed down from generation to generation. And maybe someday supply her husband with a month's worth of beer for the honeymoon (just kidding about the honeymoon thing, Cee Cee).

Later, the discussions of the menfolk turned from football to riding mowers, hot cars, and a more efficient configuration for my workbench. A field trip was in order. As we moved toward my garage, we stopped in the kitchen for another cold bottle. I paused near my carboy, looked at my sister-in-law and said, Isn't it a good-looking brew?" I couldn't make out what the look on her face meant but was sure I would see it again and again.

Cee Cee followed us to the garage; there was hope for the future.

Señor Frog's

Time has a way of getting away from us. One early spring, over a late sunny afternoon lunch with a good chum of mine from college, we reminisced over those easy days of high school and college fun. We talked about the parties, the summers full of days up at the reservoir whiling the time away on inner tubes as the waves from speedboats pushed us in and out of lazy, sun-drenched coves. We reminisced about jumping off the cliffs into the blue water below and sunning ourselves on the beach with a throng of other young party-goers. We recollected nights working in our respective taverns, when our jobs could be left behind when we left at the end of our shifts.

☆

With the crisp of the oncoming autumn, sweatshirts and sweaters were pulled out of suitcases and pulled on until the weak sun attempted to heat the afternoon air enough to don T-shirts and shorts again. Soon the cool snap would turn cold and snow would cover the campus walks. In less than a week we'd all be cracking open thick textbooks, so we enjoyed our last moments of freedom with gusto. There were kegger parties to attend, people to meet, and a rich social life to consider.

Autumn faded all too quickly, followed by a long, seemingly endless winter of studying and working; spring break couldn't come soon enough. Though there would be tough days of final exams when we returned, the break would be totally necessary.

Spring fever started up in full force, and the lucky elite on campus were filled with senioritis. Flowers sprouted and the hint of green was tingeing the lawns. The stretching college campus was tantamount to the awakening of a hill of hibernating ants. Frisbees and baseballs returned, students sprinkled the lawns on beach towels, all welcoming the sun back from its winter vacation home.

Flyers appeared everywhere, enticing college students to venture to the land of sun, fun, and a week away from all books, professors, and classes. Mazatlan, Mexico: By plane or by train, paradise could be had for a relatively small price. I put in for extra shifts at the tavern where I earned much of my tuition, board, and books. I wanted to fly with some of my dormitory gang instead of cramming in like a bunch of sardines on the train, which would eat up precious days of sun fun.

We, a group of six freshmen guys, reserved a suite at a fancy beachfront hotel before we left. None of us could afford to rent such luxury on our own. So we decided to pool our resources together for a large room with a big common area where we traded off sleeping nights on the floor, alternating to the beds in a simple system devised by the accounting major among us.

After riding from the airport to our hotel, we were excited to discover a good-sized refrigerator in the room. The six of us stripped down quickly, donning swim shorts, and ran down to the beach looking like six albino animals in relation to the others who had been there absorbing the sun's rays. We bodysurfed in the jade-colored surf, threw Frisbees and each other into the pounding waves. We played in the ocean until we were all exhausted and thirsty and then decided it was surely "beer-thirty" in Mexico.

We walked down the beach just a little ways to a gathering place of students. Right on the beach was a shrimp and beer shack. The tiny, cheerful, dark-skinned man who ran it spoke broken English, enough to handle the exchange of money for his goods with the partying gringos from the north. The shack was backed up against a large retaining wall protecting the road from hurricane waves. As we all stepped up to order a cold Mexican beer with lime, we noticed numerous stacks of cases of beer behind the shack in a makeshift fenced-off area. One of my friends spoke enough Spanish to negotiate a good deal with the man. In an instant the man went from retailer to wholesaler. We ran back to the hotel room to retrieve a ridiculously low amount of pesos for the golden nectar and carted off six cases of beer. We had enough Negro Modelo, Pacifico, and Carte Blanca to host our own little party in our luxury suite: one case per roommate for the equivalent of five dollars each. We would alternate, taking turns as five baked and played in the sun on the beach; one, in round robin fashion, would run to the room for a six-pack to refresh the group. With the hot sun of Mexico we would return to the shrimp shack several times.

Refreshed by the newly acquired beer, we headed back to the beach until the sun started sinking low into the ocean. Then our thoughts turned to nightlife and dinner. One of the popular spring break hangouts was called the Shrimp Bucket, where we could get fist-sized prawns and buckets of beer for a reasonable price. It was reputed to be one of the best hotspots in Mazatlan and wasn't far from the famous Señor Frog's, where we intended to drink margaritas, *cervezas,* and dance on the tables into the wee hours of the morning. I was the only one in the group with a steady girlfriend back home; the rest of the guys had one thing in mind other than the Mexican beer, so I forced myself to sight-see the tanned coeds along with them.

We jumped into a cab and headed to the Shrimp Bucket to start out the evening. We ordered shrimp dishes and mucho buckets of *cerveza* and waited … and waited … and waited. We soon realized that all of the wait staff were young, handsome men, who spent most of their effort on the young women at their tables. The young American women held more reason to hustle than a group of six gringos with ridiculously lobster-red-tinted skin. We complained to the manager, to which he snapped back something none of us totally under-stood, save his tone of voice. After we were served our second or third round of *cerveza* we finally got our dinners and quick-ly reordered more *cerveza*, expecting to wait. We wolfed down the shrimp dinners (the shrimp more the size of a thumb than a fist) and pounded down the next bucket of beer.

The suggestion was made that it was certainly time for us to move on to our next destination, having seen the line that had formed outside of Señor Frog's. We did everything possible to get our waiter's attention, except to jump in his path and knock the tray out of his hand. Then he sat down at a table with a large group of girls with thick Texan accents who gig-gled at everything he said in his broken and seemingly rehearsed English. Meanwhile, we waited and waited some more to pay for our tab. After what seemed like an eternity to a bunch of college guys, the suggestion was made that we give it five more minutes and if he still didn't come to the table we would bolt; we would dine and dash. We devised a plan.

The time elapsed and the four bravest of our group headed toward the door. When the final two joined us just outside the door, we all suddenly panicked and started running. As we recounted the worst stories we had all heard about Americans landing in Mexican jails, further panic struck at our stupidity. We must have looked like the six stooges, bumping into each other in our frenzy to disappear. We started sprinting out of the hamlet and onto the main highway that followed along the beach, sadly watching the bright nightlife fading behind us but bolstered by the fact that on the other end of the strip were more clubs. We would just have to go to Señor Frog's the next night.

It had been at least a ten-minute cab ride from our hotel to the restaurant, so we figured we would need to really hoof it back to avert a sure arrest. At one point there was a break along the beach wall where we discussed jumping; following along the beach, no one would know we were there. By now all logic had escaped us. We were in such a panic that we just sprinted as hard as we could. Cars whizzed by honking, and we heard a few catcalls. Two of the guys in the back of our comedic formation tried to flag down every cab driver who zoomed by, hoping we could catch a cab and totally disappear, but the cabs were all stuffed with vacationing spring breakers on their way to their next hotspot destination.

We continued to run and when the roofline of our hotel came in to view, we began to laugh with relief. We were almost home free; we were going to get away with it. One of the guys near the back of our pack, still trying to wave over a cab, finally succeeded in getting attention. The cab driver quickly moved over onto the shoulder of the road. Now that we had a cab, in less than five minutes we would be in one of the chic clubs we had heard about past hotel row, far from the Shrimp Bucket. The sheer adrenaline coursing through our veins at that point could have propelled us to run another ten miles.

The cab driver had a huge smile on his face and as we all huddled nearer the car, it was then that we noticed a man sitting in the back seat. It was the manager we had complained to at the Shrimp Bucket. Our hearts collectively sank—we were surely going to jail now. He held restaurant slips in his hand and started blustering about *la policia* and other things that seemed like the death sentence of our days of fun in the sun and possibly worse. Waving the slips, he stepped out of the cab as the one guy among us who could speak a little Spanish tried to calm him down. The cab driver, who did speak some English, explained that the manager had already called the police and that we would all surely be locked up if we didn't make good on our dinner checks. Our minimally Spanish-speaking pal bartered with the manager, and soon every one of us emptied our pockets, literally, showing the manager that we were giving him everything we had.

That dinner cost us about six times more than it would have had we summoned the manager to take our bill back at the restaurant rather than dine and dash, but we gladly paid him off to stay out of jail. As our hearts pounded loudly enough for us to almost hear them on the busy highway, the manager jumped back into the cab and the cab driver whipped across the lane and headed back to the restaurant. As they drove off, we could hear them both howling with laughter at "the stupido gringos" as I imagined the cab driver getting one of his best tips ever. They had just pulled a royal scam on us and there was nothing at all we could do about it. We were all so relieved not to be going to jail, we would have paid even more for the terrible service had we had it in our pockets.

Too poor to return to town for the night, and now having to think about a few less nights out, we walked back to our luxury hotel suite. But all was not lost. We still had our cases of cold beer in the refrigerator and there was a report of a new busload of girls from California just down the hall for my friends, so we could just have our own party in the room. Alas, we all joined in with the reveling again in the hall and rooms, and by the end of the night we, too, were retelling and laughing about the experience at the Shrimp Bucket.

We did make it to Señor Frog's the next night and several after. For the moment all worries were suspended. Jobs back home and finals soon approaching took a backseat to youthful fun.

Crowded Rooms

Some time ago, I spent a week visiting my father at a drug and alcohol rehabilitation center. I was there to support him and to try to help him deal with the difficulties he would go through getting sober and getting a better handle on his life. Since Mom had died, he turned to booze for solace. While there I endured meeting after meeting, testimonial after testimonial, about how alcohol and drugs had nearly destroyed the lives of many of the patients there, not to mention the lives of those close to them. Frankly, at times it was enough to make me want a drink. The myriad issues that robbed these people of their potential and destroyed relationships, careers, and lives was more than I wanted to deal with.

Though alcoholism itself is very serious, the issue of taking responsibility for oneself is serious as well, and I felt at times like slapping some of these people back into reality. I wanted to yell, "Stop blaming your drinking on the alcohol, blame yourself, take responsibility for your actions!" But I didn't. I just endured the meetings and chuckled later at some of the ridiculous admissions people were willing to make in the crowded rooms of strangers. All of them played the game of "top that testimony" in an attempt to swing the best tale of the evening. Amazing to me that if half of what I had heard was in fact nonfiction, these were some really whacked-out people. All of them in complicity seemed intent on pulling one over on the counselor in charge. Some of the stories told were tragic and others humorous and light, intermixed oddly with much sorrow and loss. In the meanwhile we, an assortment of family members, were all there apparently to deal with our own issues brought on by having a loved one with a substance abuse problem. My reason, so I thought, was to show my loved one the reasons to regain sobriety, to return to the daily, "normal" life, to heal.

One memory will forever stand out in my mind as the day when levity prevailed and a minor breakthrough occurred as a result of simple laughter. I'd been there for several days and was really feeling the oppressive weight of the burdens shared by all. The mood was—no pun intended—very sober and somber. I forced myself into out-of-body experiences, my imagination drifting away mercifully during the "revelation sessions" we family members attended twice daily, when a member of the group would, with too much excruciating detail, tell how their loved one had damaged them because of their own particular vice. I noticed the banner with the Twelve-Step Program hung everywhere. I made up mantras: "God grant me the serenity not to scream while someone else is talking. To not cover my ears with both hands and singsong la, la, la, to drown out the current story. To not bring a drink into these sessions in an attempt to get kicked out." The self-pity was wearing me out.

Higher powers were being evoked and I wondered which crutch some were picking up when turning in the crutch of their addiction. In every room there were reminders of sobriety, and I began to make up my own twelve steps for escaping the compound. Many times I just wanted to find the exit door and get the hell out. The counselor assigned to my group said that I was "in denial," unwilling to allow my shell to be pierced, to get into the issues holding me down due to the fact that I had an alcoholic in my life. I wondered if she would miss me if during the night I stole away to get a six-pack to keep in my cabin

We were near the boundary of the pristine Rocky Mountain National Park, just outside of Estes Park, Colorado, near the Stanley Hotel where the movie *The Shining* was filmed. (I wondered if perhaps the author might not have stayed in the compound at some point and had gotten inspired by some of the wackiness there.) The rehab center was set in what had once been a hunting lodge. There were cabins for the patients, which had once housed hunters, now drunks and druggies. The main lodge had previously been the house where a rich and philanthropic transplanted Texan hunter had lived. When the land was given to the current rehab center, the entire house was full of animal trophies intact from all over the world. On every wall some kind of animal head or pelt was displayed—deer, elk, zebra, birds of all sizes, assorted animals from Africa and many other places. A testimonial to someone with an addiction to kill every species on earth.

When a new patient arrived they were placed in isolation in a room above the main room in the lodge. One evening, I was in the lodge reading a magazine while waiting for dinner with everyone else when a new patient was brought in. He was still obviously under the influence of his vice, and I would soon learn that he had the nasty habit of mixing brandy with whatever drug was available. He came in noisily, as though he had just arrived at another party. He walked in holding a windbreaker over his head, like a star avoiding paparazzi. He was seated near me temporarily with a clear view of the entire lodge and the hundreds of animals that stared at him blankly, flanked by counselors there to keep him from bolting and disappearing in the dense forest surrounding. He took the windbreaker off his head and looked around, blinking hard. As he focused with the light change, he looked at the walls with all of those accusing, vacant, glass eyes staring at him, staggered toward a couch across from where I sat, and collapsed into the cushions exclaiming loudly, "Oh, shit! The zoo is gonna be pissed as hell when they see this!" Everyone just burst out laughing in comic relief.

That night at dinner people seemed to take things and themselves a little less seriously, a little less "sober"; humor could be the key to healing. I watched my dad chuckling over the scene again and again during the evening.

Every day I listened to stories of other people's problems with substance abuse, primarily alcohol. It was amazing to me what length some would go to to assure a totally screwed-up existence. I had never been closer to a group therapy session than enjoying the inane discourse of Bob Newhart's charges in his popular show on television that I watched in college to play a popular drinking game, the Bob Show. If you've never played, let me explain. Each person in the show prefaced every third line with the word *Bob,* as primarily everyone interacted with Bob, the psychologist. When his name was said, you chugged a beer—I think in the average show the name Bob was used twenty-five to fifty times, Very good drinking game fodder, eh?

Anyway, I wasn't prepared personally for the Al-Anon procedure of working through the healing process toward forgiving the person who had wronged us with his or her addictions. Common stories were shared by other family members present, embarrassing moments, humiliation and shame revealed as a result of our loved one's vices. I was being sucked into the vacuum of self-pity and began to revel in that pit when our counselor pulled us out and told us it was time to stand on our own two feet, to cast off all denial, and to live more freely. Confronted by demons I didn't know were lurking beneath the surface of my psyche, I was challenged to take account of where some of my ideas, insecurities, and other assorted maladies had taken a foothold and was thus challenged further to excise them. Generally finding much of modern psychology and theories of dysfunction to be psychobabble, the healthy skeptic in me arose. Half the time I wanted to laugh and half the time I wanted to cry.

A revelation occurred for me about midweek outside of all of the therapy sessions. I was taking a walk around the compound with my dad, a comical circle where patients and their loved ones tread, observing the strict boundaries rules. The track around the compound was the outer boundary and each patient spent time on the edge of it as often as possible. It was like a moving *Cuckoo's Nest* scene. We were walking and talking about what was going on there when the conversation turned to what had brought us there. I looked into the sad eyes of my father as he explained how painful it was to have lost his wife. How life was so desperately lonely without her, and with very little comfort to be found he had found what comfort he could.

My heart broke when she died, too. I chose to bury myself in my occupation and my family; my father chose to find an escape from his pain with friends like Jack Daniels and Jim Beam. Who could blame him? Loneliness robs a person of will.

Without the will to carry on, the abuse of anything medicating the pain is more understandable.

Our conversation turned to other things, specifically about our relationship and where it would go from there. As we loosened up and shared our pain, dreams, and thoughts about what had happened and would happen now, a question welled up that I somehow always knew was there but had suppressed for many years. My friends and I had talked about the strange dance of relationship with a dad when one is an adult. So many of my male friends had slipped away from a relationship with their dads once they gained independence, yet stayed close to their moms. As though I had no control over the welling question, it came out …

"Dad, do you like me?"

He looked at me quizzically, as though the question was ridiculous, and then started nodding. The recognition that the same question remained between him and his own dad who was long gone was apparent to both of us. His eyes welled.

I jumped in before he could answer. "I mean, I know you love me and all, but do you like me?" I felt bad, thinking of how much he was going through; here I was adding more.

He took a deep breath. "I like you very much … it makes me sad that you have to ask."

I swallowed hard. "It's important to me."

"Is this something new?" he asked flinchingly.

"I guess I've never really known," I said honestly.

"I do like you. I like so much about you."

I felt my heart warm. Doubt flooded away, filling me with something lasting that changed me fundamentally right there. "I like you, too," I said, as we joined in a warm embrace.

Later that night I wrote letters to my young sons about

how much I loved and liked them. They would never have to ask, I resolved.

My dad and I connected there in a way we never had before. I was able to walk in his proverbial moccasins for a moment and I saw him in a different light than ever before.

I understood.

I forgave.

He forgave.

We began to heal. Together.

The Neighborhood Bully

One of the fathers in the neighborhood I grew up in carried a beer literally wherever he went. When he was working on his car he had a beer in his hand. When he was mowing his lawn and the few times I ever saw him playing with his children he had a beer in his hand. I remember the man as though a can of beer was little more than an extension of his hand. The other hand I remember unfortunately as the one that doled out painful slaps to the head, a perfect match for his acid tongue, his children the unhappy recipients of both. His numerous, daily beers were drunk mostly in solitude, usually while working in his garage in the same manner a chain smoker uses when lighting the next one with the butt of the previous one. I remember avoiding him mostly because of his arrogant and often angry attitude. His three sons were my constant childhood companions, particularly the middle son, Franky, who was closet in age to me. I always knew their father's attitude and anger inhabited much of their waking thoughts and that they feared him more than anything else.

We lived out in the country and my unfortunate friends often occupied themselves by the many streams, fields, lakes, trees, and other ways to stay away from home during the day. Even as a young boy, I sensed that their father's behavior had something to do with the numerous empty beer cans that constantly littered the floor of their garage.

Franky's beer-swilling father remained totally silent toward me until one day he decided to "bless" me by sharing with me a piece of his sage wisdom and mercifully brief companionship. I was twelve years old and we had gathered at Franky's house to play basketball. His malevolent father, who usually puttered about in the garage working on some machine or another, totally ignoring us, came out of the garage and dully watched us as we attempted to hit the backboard with an under-inflated basketball. He barked at Franky to go get him another can of beer. My companion scurried into the house to avoid the sure punishment he would receive if he delayed. I remember my brother's face as he flashed me a look of near horror. Franky's brothers hardly flinched, used to it, probably relieved at not being singled out for once. I remember thinking it must be a mixed feeling to be the one to retrieve the substance that might ensure your own abuse.

The father from hell had an extended, whitened belly like a huge pregnant fish, greased hair combed straight back, and a wide face. He stood there in the driveway scratching his enormous, hairy, blanched belly, then belched and looked over my way. Fear gripped my insides, as I was sure he wanted to lay a blow to the side of my head, too. He stepped over to me, looked into my eyes with the most kindly look I had ever seen on his face. He belched, and blowing his caustic breath out sideways did the oddest thing—he put his arm around my shoulder and drew me close to his sweating, fish-belly-white stomach. The man had never spoken to me, had never even so much as acknowledged my presence before, save a nasty look here and there. I remember not knowing what to do, sweat and terror creeping across my body like a snake. I stood shaking slightly with anticipation of his next dreaded move.

Franky delivered the can of beer, which must have been his father's fifth or sixth by then, and looked astonished at his father's familiarity with me. The man eased me into a headlock as he brought his hamlike fists together to open the can, popped it open, yanked gently on my neck with his floppy arm and then said, "Kid, remember what I tell you now; it's important." He pulled on my shoulder tight with his free hand as he attempted to drain the first half of the can of beer in one gulp. I stood there simply petrified, awaiting his words. He belched again, blew it out, and chuckled. The smug look on his face indicated that he was about to release the wisdom of the ages. I could smell the sour scent of beer on his breath as he leaned his face toward mine and intently stated, "When the frost is on the pumpkin, then it's time for peter dunkin." He laughed far too hard, released me, and went back to work on his refrigerator parts in the garage.

I stood there still shaking. I had no idea what he meant by the comment. The whole group of boys stood there speechless, the sons of the neighborhood bully embarrassed and lacking words. The game soon moved to safer territory when the older boys explained what their father was saying. It was so out of context and such a stupid thing to say. I forever associated his ridiculous behavior with his drinking.

He never said another word to me, for which I have always been eternally grateful. Those words stuck with me for some strange reason as I pondered why he had singled me out for them. Although I would have rather just forgotten him and his dumb little saying, some things just stick with you. The whole neighborhood knew of the abuse taking place in that house, but back then sadly you didn't say anything; one didn't interfere. If that man behaved the same way nowadays, the children would likely be removed from his "cave."

Several years later the family moved away. My father always remarked that he felt sorry for those kids and that someday their father would feel remorse for his treatment of them. Years later, when I was in high school, I heard that the oldest boy, the one the father had always seemed roughest on, was in a boy's home or a detention center of some sort for stealing a car while drunk and underage. I wasn't at all surprised to hear it. How unfortunate, though, that no one had ever locked up his abusive father before it was too late for his sons.

As an adult now, I can view that experience through different eyes. The mix of anger when propelled by a constant stream of alcohol is extremely dangerous. Strangely, it is often the negative experiences that shape the adult a child will become. Shortly after becoming a father, I vowed that my children would never see their father intoxicated to the point of such stupidity. Franky's father has always been the symbol of a father I would never become.

Going Postal

My wife and I grew up in Colorado, rare natives. But when we got married we wanted to establish our independence, so we moved—of all unlikely places for mountain-loving, Colorado-bred-and-born people—to Texas. Mercifully, we moved to Austin where the rolling hills, lush green vegetation, and overall warm people flourish, and the surrounding hills were a reminder of home. We found a nice apartment, nestled into the woods, and set up house and our new lives.

Not long after moving into our new abode we started noticing something strange in the middle of the night. There was a loud knock-knocking—repetitive and annoying—like a human-sized woodpecker intent on a wall somewhere. It was the kind of noise that wakes you up in the middle of the night and renders you unable to fall back asleep for a while because your imagination runs wild to its origin.

After a week of the nocturnal noise, I could take it no longer and slipped into some shorts, exploring the outside of the apartment complex we lived in for signs of the noisemaker.

Nothing in site was causing the ruckus and when I returned to my bed the noise had stopped. Several nights later it started up again. We sat there in the dark listening intently, trying to figure out where the noise was coming from. Then we listened hard enough to hear other noises mixing with the knock-knocking sound that was keeping us from our sleep. The human noises accompanying indicated that the knocking sound was coming from the apartment below us. We concluded that it was caused by possibly another couple recently married and intent on filling the jar on the nightstand with pennies their first year, to which it is reputed you would spend the rest of your life removing them. I resolved to do nothing, knowing the noise would soon subside. I had yet to meet our neighbors and didn't want to do so in the middle of the night over something potentially embarrassing for both of us.

I had the next day off from work, and as my wife prepared to go teach her classroom full of kids we talked about what I should do to try to resolve our middle-of-the-night issue so we could go back to sleeping. I told her I'd introduce myself to our neighbor and see if somehow I could work the issue of the night sounds into our conversation in a way that would cause little to no conflict. Later, I heard the door to the apartment below ours open and then close. I walked out onto the landing in front of our apartment and watched a pretty young woman leaving. I went back into our apartment and could hear the sounds of her husband stirring below and resolved to go to the pool and talk to him midmorning.

After a nice swim in the sweltering August heat I retreated to the air conditioning of our apartment. I heard music downstairs and thought it was as good a time as any to try to broach the nocturnal subject at hand. I stood at the door of my downstairs neighbor's apartment with a small knot in my stomach wondering how I was going to make this easy and avoid conflict. My wife would have baked cookies to welcome them or introduce herself first to somehow buffer the issue. My wife wasn't here nor would she have brought up the knocking in a first conversation, but I was desperate for an uninterrupted night of sleep. I knocked again harder to be heard over the booming base of my neighbor's music. I heard someone step to the door and then it opened. There stood a very large black man with a protruding belly and boxer shorts on. A cat with full and extended nipples suddenly squished out between his large foot and the door jam. He cursed loudly at it. "Damn cat! Come back here!"

I looked at him curiously. He explained that the cat was nursing five kittens but getting sick of them, and every time the door opened he had to guard it from her darting out. I heard Johnny Mathis now crooning in the background and the soft mewing of five kittens stuffed inside a small apartment that didn't allow pets under any circumstances. He looked at me and muttered, "I hain't interested," and started to back into his apartment, ready to shut the door. A shiny gold tooth right in the front of his mouth added to the overall impression of a big man who wanted to be left alone. I felt a chill crawl up my spine and wished I could find a graceful way back to my own apartment, reasoning that this was an insane mission. This man was in no mood to talk to a stranger, and bringing up the delicate subject of his middle-of-the-night, noisy wall-thumping lovemaking was the last thing I wanted to do right then.

I must have looked baffled because as he was closing the door, he asked me what it was that I was selling. I explained that I wasn't selling anything, that I lived right above him. He invited me in, periodically glancing out the window at the parking lot for signs of the cat returning or the manager noticing the pet. He apologized, explaining that he was grouchy because he worked the swing shift and had had a rather rough night. I wondered which part he considered rough but kept my comments to myself. He was in the postal service and he always got home around two o'clock in the morning. I reasoned that he must shed his clothes then get right to business with his wife because it was about then that I was awakened every other night like clockwork. He invited me into his tiny kitchen for a cup of coffee.

"Name's Dell." He extended a huge hand to shake mine. We sat down together and talked about his job, where I had come from (he noticed my lack of accent?), and other topical issues. Two of the kittens gathered around me, jumping up into my lap and then curling around my feet, playing with my shoestrings and batting at each other, providing welcome relief from staring into my neighbor's bleary morning eyes.

I looked around, surveying the layout of his apartment, realizing it was the identical layout to mine, which meant that our bedrooms were aligned perfectly. I leaned forward spying into his bedroom as he retrieved himself another cup of coffee and saw that sure enough, his bed was set right under ours, the headboard right up against the wall, the culprit of my lack of sleep. He stood, stretched, and changed the record on his turntable from Johnny Mathis to Aretha Franklin, then settled back down at the kitchen table eyeing me warily.

I tried to get a sense of how he might take my request, which I had resolved was basically easy but potentially embarrassing. Then I thought of how sex wasn't embarrassing to men, usually more of a badge of pride and that he would probably be just fine with my bringing it up. We'd be just like two guys sitting at a bar or snapping towels in the locker room after discussing the manly conquests (sex in the middle of the

night, the louder the better, and the manlier the brag after all).
Somewhere in our conversation I asked if he was a newlywed
to which he smirked and nodded.

Then I just decided to come out with it, ban the diplo-
macy act and niceties—we were talking about sleep here.
"Dell, do you think you could move your bed away from the
wall?" I said this with all of the subtlety of a rhino making
ketchup in a tomato garden. He looked at me through blood-
shot eyes and I thought he was going to stand up and pound on
me by the look on his face. Every story I had ever heard of
postal workers going postal came to me in an instant blur.
Suddenly a wide smile crossed his face as it registered what I
was asking. I felt a great relief when that big gold tooth
appeared as his grin continued to widen. I started to laugh and
explain how the headboard must be slamming against the wall.
(Oh, how powerful you must be, you testosterone-filled lad.)
How the bed was right underneath where we slept and I wondered if he couldn't just move it a few inches toward the middle of the room so we could *all* enjoy the evening more. He
started to laugh, a deep Barry White laugh, his voice so deep
that when he laughed it was almost creepy.

Locker room talk, bonding stuff, surely we would
have a good laugh out of this one now and every time we
bumped into each other in the hall or the pool; we would just
wink, we would have a history to support our newfound
friendship. Dell let out a big belly laugh, his voice raised at
least four octaves from Barry White to that guy Jimmy Walker
who used to say, "DYNOMITE!" all the time, and Dell said,
"Whoo boy, don't ever tell Desiree this—she would just rightly
die. Oh yeah, she would!"

Back to Barry White chuckling as he rubbed his
ample stomach with male pride. I could tell he was anxious to

tell her himself. He couldn't wait to spill the goods, somehow anticipating the joke they would share. I was quite relieved that Dell was taking this so well and thought it must surely be time for me to go. I moved the tiny kitten off of my lap; she had made herself a little nest and had gone to sleep. I looked up at the clock on the wall and commented how the morning had just gotten away from me and that I still had a ton of things to do.

Dell leaned over with his silky Barry White voice and said, "So, you are from Colorado, huh? You have any good barbecue up there?" his big gold tooth gleamed from his smiling mouth and his hand found his stomach again as if to remember the barbecue.

I said, "Yeah, some."

And he chuckled too loudly and said, "But not like down here! You said it was your day off, didn't you? You wanna have some good barbecue and brews for lunch with me?" His thick Southern accent indicated to me that he had come from one of the southeastern states, possibly Alabama or Louisiana. I detected a slight Cajun lilt and pieced together the possibilities.

Because my wife and I didn't have any friends in Austin yet, I reasoned it would be a nice thing to have Dell as a friend. He seemed a good type, like he could have a fun sense of humor—and after all, he had taken what I requested quite well, actually even found it amusing. So I said I would go take a shower to get the chlorine from the pool off of me and then we could go. As I headed out his front door, he pointed at the two kittens that seemed to take a liking to me and said, "We are giving those away now. You want 'em?"

I thought to myself, *Yeah, that's all we need to get evicted in Austin with nowhere to go. Maybe we could move in with Dell and the missus and bang the walls in unison.*

A short time later, I met Dell downstairs at his door. He grabbed his car keys, explaining that he would drive because he knew where to go. He said he was going to take me to a place where they made the best barbecue on earth, a place like no other I'd been to. He told me as we headed out of Austin proper that Lyndon Johnson had loved this place and actually had their barbecue delivered to the White House when he was president.

Dell talked eagerly about how the meat fell off the bones, how just thinking about getting that barbecue "fix" made his mouth water. From the looks of him, his fixes were more frequent than not. He made me hungry just thinking about it. He talked about how a Lone Star beer on a hot summer day with the greatest barbecue in the world could make a man feel like he died and went to heaven. That there was only one thing he liked better than barbecue and a beer, to which he winked, showed me that gold tooth again, and I acknowledged that I knew where he was going with that. *Just move the headboard, Dell,* I thought to myself.

We drove out of the city, and through miles and miles of the humid plains I watched the great city of Austin disappear behind them. Our windows were rolled down as the hot, sticky air swirled about us thick and stifling. Dell kept glancing nervously over in my direction, possibly, like me, realizing we had no history. We had nothing really in common yet except our shared knowledge of nighttime noises, and so the conversation seemed strained for the time being. My imagination started to capture me, realizing I hadn't left a note for my wife in the event that we got home late. My car was sitting in front of the apartment, and there was no sign of where I had gone, leaving a total mystery to my whereabouts if I disappeared into thin air. As my mind wandered, trying to think of something to say, I started to imagine the strangest things. I had perhaps read one too many killer thrillers, but suddenly the looks Dell was nervously flashing in my direction took on a strange feel.

Thirty minutes later with no end to our drive in sight, I started wondering if telling Dell, a complete stranger, to move his bed away from the wall was such a keen idea. We seemed to be getting a little too far from the city to really be going to lunch. My imagination started to grip me more; the first tinge of fear started to gnaw at my stomach. The humidity and heat was almost unbearable as the hot wind whipped in and out of the window in thick swirls. When I asked Dell if we were getting close—he by this time had given up trying to compete with the loud sound of the swirling wind in the car and apparently had no use for the air conditioner—was hum-singing loudly in his deep baritone Barry White voice to an early form of rap/soul music I didn't recognize.

I asked again over the loud cacophony of sounds if we were almost there. He smiled and tapped his finger to the windshield as if to say just a few more minutes. By this time my imagination had completely taken over, and I had a full-blown scenario in mind of just how Dell would dispose of my body. I measured how soft the shoulder of the road would be to jump out and roll when Dell's tapping on the windshield again brought me out of my ridiculous trance.

After what seemed like hours we entered a tiny town, the kind of town where you can spit with a good wind from one side to the other. Dell passed right through it, and my hope that we had finally arrived diminished as we hit yet another endless band of asphalt. There was little in sight save the huddles of cows every few miles, a few rabbits, and the drying husks of armadillos baking in the sun on the side of the road. Dell started to tap on the windshield again, showing me another upcoming "spit and miss" Texas town.

He suddenly pulled the car over onto the shoulder of the road and deftly headed into a little graveyard (I swear this is true). I looked at him with what must have been terror and at this point a sense of curiosity. I wondered if the people who lived in this little town ever made it to the big city and how this place had to do with getting a barbecue lunch. He said, "There's something in here you just gotta see."

As he drove to the very back of the graveyard we entered a small enclave of trees huddled in what looked to be a long, oblong circle totally hidden from view from the highway or any other living soul. I figured my suspicions had been right. Dell looked over at me and the sun caught the gold on his tooth, and I half expected him to reach for a machete or something else to do me in with. My hand reached for the door handle as I planned my escape. I suddenly wondered if Dell had come from Alabama at all or if he had grown up just yonder a few miles from the graveyard. I wondered if he had made up for the boredom of small-town living in the middle of nowhere by catching stranded motorists or those others lulled into the whole barbecue pitch. Was this some kind of a homecoming for him for a guy who had insulted him just hours before who now would get his just dessert, already conveniently in a graveyard?

Dell walked over to the back of the enclave and waved for me to follow, which I did obediently, reasoning surely I was just letting my imagination get the best of me. I eyed him again, figuring with his bulk I could outrun him pretty easy, flag down a passing trucker, and get to the next town if I needed to. I would just stay at arms' length in case. As I neared the place he was looking at I saw what we were there for. Standing in front of us was a miniature replica of a small Texas town, much like those I had seen coming to and from Austin and in Old West books. The miniature buildings represented what once was all Texas and in many places still existed. The place reminded Dell of his hometown, he said. It really was a wonder how the miniatures looked so real and at the back of the old cemetery seemed a worthy tourist attraction, enough of a reason to divert off the road on the way to lunch with a new friend. I wondered how in the hell he had ever found this little town, but I had asked enough questions and pried into his personal affairs enough.

When Dell stood tall and slapped me on the back and said, "Whatcha say we get some of that supper now?" I thought I would laugh so hard I'd cry. It was only then that I realized how much my stupid imagination had gotten away from me and how relieved I felt to know Dell wasn't planning my demise after all but was being a good ol' Texas tourist guide.

Soon, Dell and I sat in the old brick-lined building with thick, black soot painting the interior walls from the huge ovens and the delicious scent of tangy barbecue emanating from the entire place. An old heavyset woman, with floppy upper arms in a muumuu dress, set two large sheets of butcher paper in front of us. In no time she covered them in spicy sausage, ribs, beef strips, pork strips, potato salad, and beans with a large cup of tangy barbecue sauce each, and then she set two huge ice-frosted mugs of golden beer in front of us.

Dell lifted his mug and motioned for me to do the same before the frost turned to water on the table. He said loud enough for the whole town to hear, "Liquid bread! Texas toast! This whole plate! I'll eat, I boast!" It wasn't a prayer but we were thankful enough. I was tempted to drink an entire six-pack to alleviate the stress I had felt on the way out to "supper." We clinked our glasses together and toasted to new friendship, to a chance, noisy, middle-of-the-night encounter that had brought us together, to this place, and then we toasted our wives.

"Mmm, mmm, mmm, that Desiree of mine is allllll woman!" Dell gave me a sly wink and I wondered if it bothered him that I knew much more about his wife than he knew about mine. The heat in the restaurant matched the heat outside so we poured the beer down our throats and ordered several more while we tore into the most tender, delicious barbecue I had ever eaten before or since. Dell was right—the home-grown Lone Star beer on a hot, humid, terror-filled August afternoon was the best-tasting beer I'd had in Texas. It was definitely worth the drive.

On the way back with more ease behind us, I started to relate how my imagination had gotten away from me and how it felt when Dell had pulled into the graveyard. He got a great laugh out of that, made some comment about "going postal," and then looked at me in earnest, with the gold tooth and said in his thick Barry voice, "Well, we ain't home yet," then thumped my leg and we laughed most of the way back home.

Sometime a few nights later, in the middle of the night, I heard a bumping sound and thought, they'd moved the bed back next to the wall without knowing it in their passionate frenzy. I looked at the digital clock, it was only midnight, and Dell wouldn't be home for several hours yet. Still there was a noise, but it was different. This time it was in our apartment. I walked slowly toward the noise and then in the moonlight I saw the two kittens, Mathis and Aretha, tossing each other about. Dell had insisted we accept his gift of the two kittens and who was I to argue with my new friend after all we'd been through already?

Though my relationship with Dell started tenuously, humorously, and felt much like a *Twilight Zone* episode, I soon learned that he and Desiree were good folks to know. I hope all these years later they are still moving the four-poster bed to Johnny Mathis in a nocturnal embrace.

Imagine That

Imagine being able to just drop what you're doing and live your ultimate dream job, dream life. What would it be? Would it be many things? Where would you start? Imagine being able to follow your passion(s) completely, to have someone or something else supply the conduit to your dreams. Like winning the lottery. They say money doesn't change people for the better. Yet I have lived with money and without it, and although through both experiences I was basically the same person, money enabled experiences that otherwise would not have been possible.

I have always dreamed of having a quaint place in a quaint town, and even more so the dream includes living overseas. I was recently sharing a pint and a good Mexican meal with a friend when he told me about something he had just read about in the newspaper that was right up my dream ally. Apparently one of my favorite brewers gives away a pub every year, and this year they were giving one away in Ireland. The winner would become a "publican" and would take title to his or her own pub. All you had to do was enter with a fifty-word-or-less essay starting with "The perfect pint of Guinness is ..." and you stood a chance of being selected as a finalist and then possibly a publican.

"What better way to blend your passions for writing, beer, and travel," my friend explained, "than to run your own pub in Ireland, and to have the atmosphere and experiences to continue to write."

I went home straight away, found the Guinness Web site, and read the rules. I read about the previous winners and how their lives of relative mundane endeavors had changed. The winner the year before was a young man with an Irish name, which made me think to enter under Justin O'Matott. He had been in a some marketing job in Manhattan and gave it all up to become a publican. Shortly after he won, an article appeared in the newspaper showing him surrounded by warm, smiling, Irish faces in front of his new pub. He had apparently been welcomed with open arms into his new life and I thought *Now, that is what I want.* Other winners included retirees, people looking for second careers, or like me—who just thought the dream was worth pursuing.

Some winners apparently had sold their pubs since, but it appeared that most had made the move over, allowing the lifestyle change to inhabit their lives. I felt a great sense of envy. I imagined what St. Patrick's Day must mean for a publican in Ireland. I thought of all of the pubs that I had visited while in Britain. I remembered watching the movie *Waking Ned Devine* and being so enamored with the pub-gathering scenes. Wishing to be a part of the celebrations that took place in the tiny Irish town in the tiny Irish pub, I started to long for the life there.

After daydreaming about what it would mean to win, I began to compose some essays on a scratch pad. I gathered a stout from the icebox, ceremoniously and somewhat super-stitiously filled my Guinness mug, and went to the sunny patch on my front porch and started jotting down essay ideas. Nearly two hours later, having been totally lost in my exalta-tions about the flavor, ambiance, dreams, and wonder of pos-sibilities, I had my essays ready to enter. I found no real guid-ance for what the Guinness people were looking for. The only hint I found was the article quoting last year's winner as say-ing no idea was too dumb. I thought, *Oh, yeah? Well, I'll show you dumb.*

I thought what I should do is spend the next two weeks doing nothing but submitting essay entries to the Guinness company, blocking other entries, and stuffing the ballot box, if you will. I thought if nothing else I could earn a place in their famous book for the most entries ever received for a sweepstakes contest by one desperate entrant. The same company that creates the lovely, dark, creamy, tasty (oops, sorry—still composing, I suppose) beer is the same one that publishes the famous *Guinness Book of World Records*. I would set the record for the American most desperate to win a pub.

Guinness has been a part of my life since long before I was of legal drinking age. When I was a boy, I'd ride my bike from our country home into town to Al's Newsstand to buy sev-eral magazines, candy, and when it came out the latest annual edition of the *Guinness Book of World Records.* The scent of newsprint and tobacco would overwhelm you in a wonderful way when you entered. I loved that smell—enough that I still frequent tiny newsstands just for the nostalgic pull. I'd then ride my bike over to the college campus where my parents taught and sit under a tall tree, eat my lunch, and peruse the pages of my new book. I'd marvel at the huge twin brothers riding tiny motorcycles because of their enormous combined girth. I can still see the picture of an enormously huge guy—I think his name was Hughes—standing in a pair of oversized overalls and the notation that he was buried in a piano box and hoisted by a crane into his grave. Forever burned in my mind is the eastern Indian man with the disgustingly long, curling fingernails and the tiny princess standing on a box, the records for eating and athletic feats, and on and on. I would flip from page to page, reading every entry like it was a compelling novel, wondering who might have broken some of the longer standing records. I used to dream of doing something someday to gain entrance into the book.

I signed on to the Worldwide Web and began to enter the contest for the pub, over and over again. These were some of the entries I sent in. You be the judge—would *you* give me a pub? Remember it's fifty words starting with "The perfect pint of Guinness is ..." and remember the disclaimer, no idea is too dumb.

> The perfect pint of Guinness is one that has just finished its cascade, is set upon the bar in a favorite local, then handed to a friend because the next one is coming. The glasses are then held high, clinked together, and then the toast to health, wealth, and happiness.

> The perfect pint of Guinness is so fine, tastier than the finest champagne or wine. Its dark and textured cascade is oh so true, and then what's left is it, a friend and you. So drink it down and get yourself another. With a Guinness, all men are brothers.

Independence Days

The perfect pint of Guinness is shared in front of a roaring fireplace in a ski lodge after a perfect day of skiing. The cascade within the pint a reminder of the cascading snow that just hours ago captured me, but oh, not quite like the next pint of Guinness.

The perfect pint of Guinness is now sitting in a slender can just moments away, a reminder of those lovely pulled pints of yesterday. The whoosh of the released gas and the pour into a mug I bought while in Britain. The taste and I am back again. Ah, Britannia!

The perfect pint of Guinness is the one that's in my hand. The perfect pint of Guinness is the one that just was poured. The perfect pint of Guinness is just being delivered into the back room in kegs. The perfect pint of Guinness just is. It just is perfect.

The perfect pint of Guinness is what awaits me when I move my family into my coveted pub, J. O'Sullivan's, in Newcastle. The first pint is for my wife and me and then the round I send out to anyone who comes in the door of the new publicans.

The perfect pint of Guinness is set down in front of me, still cascading, still waiting. I will wait as I have so many times before, because my father used to tell me, "The best things in life are worth waiting for." My Guinness is no exception. Thank you, Dad.

The perfect pint of Guinness is lying over the
ocean, the perfect pint is lying over the sea,
my Guinness awaits across the ocean, please
bring back my Guinness to me. For we have
spent time in Britain and it is to Britain I will
return again and again and again.

I imagined what it would be like to move my family to
Ireland. I thought I might just rent our house out and try it for
a year or two to see how the family adjusted. I thought about
the book that had been running through my mind regarding
the beers of Europe and how it would provide me with the perfect frame of mind and ability to hop to a few other countries
to research. Mostly, I thought of how wonderful it would be to
go to the land of Guinness, heather and fog. To provide my
sons with an experience unmatched by any other in my imagination, then the thought occurred to me: I would wait just long
enough to see if I won the contest and then maybe suggest to
my wife that we go anyway. But just before I brought it up, perhaps I would try the lottery.

Oh, well, there is always next year. A new year, a new
pub. For now, I will brush up on the dialect and read about all
that Ireland has to offer. Now, where are those galoshes and my
raincoat, anyway?...

Rodeo

Though my father is Ivy League educated and a holds a Ph.D., his roots have always been entrenched in the humble upbringings of his youth as a farm boy in upstate New York. He taught classical literature by day and listened to country western music by night. He frequented bars in little honky-tonk towns under the guise of research for characters within his current novel. He owned and rode his own horses. It was not unusual to wake up during the early morning hours before the sun had threatened the horizon to the soft twanging of Hank Williams, Sr.'s, crooning and the soft tap-tapping of my father's typewriter. Though an academician, my father was always more comfortable socially with those who had simpler tastes, preferring perhaps a cold glass of beer with a cowboy than a scotch in the faculty lounge.

As a teenager, I accompanied my dad to rodeo after rodeo across the plains towns of Colorado and sometimes up into Wyoming and Montana. Dad was the rodeo club adviser for the state university in my hometown. We would drive miles and miles in my dad's pickup truck, from small town to small town, to join the competitions. When I was in junior high school, I was able to hang out with college-age bull riders, barrel racers, and bronc riders where—because of their relationship to my dad—they seemed to accept me as one of them without the normal constraints of caution around one much younger. They never seemed to feel the need to censor their jokes or tone down the ever-present flirting and carrying on. One of the constants while traveling were the cases of beer the men would haul hoisted on their shoulders into the hotel rooms to be enjoyed later with a savory barbecue on the lawn of perhaps the only hotel in the tiny town.

Sometimes Dad would let me bring along a friend, often the same friend who roped me into riding a few bulls with him to catch the pretty cowgirls' eyes. Though we were too young to compete in the collegiate ranks, we joined the Little Britches Rodeo and learned the ropes from the older cowboys. We would stand out at the dusty pens looking over the stables of livestock, remarking intelligently on their size and mean reputations. Neither of us were willing to discuss just how scared we were when on the back of an angry bull that had only one thing on its mind: to destroy the person straddling it.

We tried to emulate the cowboys who would speak of each bull as though they knew everything about them; all the bulls had names and reputations. The nights before and during the college rodeo events were a chance to party and celebrate. When I went on these trips with my dad, he would usually look the other way if I sipped from the cans of beer as a barbecue was rendered.

When the college-age cowboys had had one too many of the longneck beers, they would start into a song of their own: "Show me the way to go home. I'm tired and I want to go to bed. I had me a drink about an hour ago and it went straight to my head. " My friend and I would roll our eyes at the ludicrous thought that they had actually believed it had been an hour since they had had their last drink. They had been opening one longneck after another with little pause since early evening. We also found it humorous that they were asking for directions to get home, because "home" was literally only steps away. But the more they drank their beers, the easier it was for my friend and me to pilfer a few of our own, and soon found ourselves singing a rendition of the song together with a buzz on.

We felt quite grown-up and though slightly miserable, we were even somewhat proud of the hangover feeling we had the next morning. My dad would roust us with exclamations of how good it would be to go down to the little café on Main Street and eat some greasy sausage and eggs to start the day off in the little plains town. Our stomachs would turn as we tried to pretend nothing was wrong. What I didn't know then was just how wise my dad was to our little pilfers.

There was one cowboy in the university club named Dusty, the official photographer and the country western rendition of a nerd or a geek. He was a tall, skinny young man with thick glasses. He had bucked and browned teeth from years of well water, and a huge belt buckle emblazoned with a bull that one of his pals had given him in honor of his faithful photographs, though he himself never drew nearer to a bull than a telephoto lens. He had come from some ranch up north to learn more from one of the best agriculture colleges in the country. He was a saddle-bronc rider wannabe without the courage to put into motion his desire. He was so skinny that one or two beers were more than he could tolerate. When the others had convinced him to go past his logical limit, they would hoist him up onto a makeshift bull, made from a fifty-gallon tank held between several trees, and give him the ride of his life. Before he became too inebriated to do anything but slobber down the front of his western shirt, Dusty told the meanest, funniest jokes.

One night, while staying in a new hotel in a tiny Colorado town in the middle of nowhere, which boasted of an indoor atrium with rooms looking down into the center common area, there was a loud crashing sound. Everyone got up from the bar set in the middle of the makeshift atrium to see what had happened. In his drunken state, Dusty had walked right through a glass door, shattering it completely. Except for his wounded pride and a nasty bruise on his nose and forehead, he escaped the accident unscathed.

On those nights on the road with my dad, the cowboys, and the cowgirls, I would observe the humorous interactions and learn about the ways of adults a little more. I would sit up on the second floor of the hotel with my friend, our legs pushing through the iron railing, dangling down as we listened to the crowd of rodeo clubbers singing in harmony from modern and old country songs. They toasted and roasted each others' foibles in the dusty arenas, each dreaming his name would someday be added to the famous of the professional rodeo circuit. I'd watch my dad down there with the college kids—he seemed just one of the boys. As if he were back on the farm, he enjoyed those trips "back to the country." He would swap "war stories" and laugh, as I had rarely seen him before. My friend and I sat in listening on with wonder as the men swore and told their stories. We would take what we had learned from the college cowboys back to the dusty pens of the Little Britches Rodeos.

At the end of the second summer of riding bulls in Little Britches, I drew a huge Brahma named Buckshot. Buckshot was the most dreaded bull in the pen. He was white with reddish-brown spots that looked like a spread of shotgun pellets—hence his name. He had a large hump and a terrifying set of horns that looked as though someone had filed them to needle-sharp points. My stomach dropped when I drew out ol' Buckshot. He was of course the bull my cowboy buddies had oohed and ahhed at earlier, all dreading the thought of pulling his name.

As we looked over the metal pen at the brown-caked backside of Buckshot, I got a good look at the bull who struck the most fear in the riders there. Buckshot had reportedly gored a cowboy who lost a lung, kidney, and half of the function in his legs—that was all my cowboy friends could confirm. I was afraid I would wet myself as I climbed down the chute onto Buckshot's muscled back. I started praying like I hadn't since my first communion years earlier.

Time stretched out. All I had to do was nod and the rope would be pulled to let Buckshot and me out for our eight-second dance. I saw the looks of pity on the faces of my friends surrounding my pen. When I knew too much time was elapsing and the suicide knot started to tighten too much around my hand, I gave the nod. Buckshot rocketed out of the pen, rearing forward then backward, then he began to spin in a whirling of white and brown streaks that took my breath away. The adrenaline began to surge, and I was determined to beat Buckshot at his own game.

Seconds spun out as though they were whole minutes. At four seconds, I felt my legs beginning to fly heavenward. I was bucking off, but my hand was staying on Buckshot. Terror gripped me. I was hung up. I couldn't get my hand free and all the time Buckshot was tossing me like a rag doll out of control. Two rodeo clowns ran in whooping and hollering, trying to distract Buckshot from goring me with those ten-foot horns that were growing with each second. A third clown jumped in and worked my hand free. Buckshot spun, knocking both me and my savior clown into what seemed the next county. I jumped up and ran, more like limped very fast, to the surrounding gate while the rodeo clowns herded Buckshot to the exit.

The roar in my ears began to subside and I saw that the crowd was on its feet clapping and cheering. I saw my dad with several of my buddies and my brother. He gave me a proud smile and I could see the relief on his face that I had walked away only bruised.

That was the last rodeo I would compete in. Buckshot had taught me enough to know that I was no cowboy. Over at the snack bar a neon sign flashed COORS. I wondered if Dad would let me; after all, I had earned it.

Though I haven't contemplated riding a bull for many years and many more years have passed since I last saw a rodeo, I still sometimes put on a country western CD and am transported back to that time when Buckshot almost owned me. I put on my ostrich skin cowboy boots (a yuppie, not real cowboy pair), crank up the stereo, and grab a six-pack of longnecks. As they say, "You can take the boy out of the country, but you can't take the country out of the boy." That's got to be in a song somewhere. Call it "Buckshot."

Still Just Boys

My wife and I settled into our first house, a small brick number and no palace to be sure, but it was ours. I had the closing documents and the canceled mortgage checks to prove it. Somehow when you get married young, you have a tough time letting go of some of the behaviors of a teenager. If you're lucky you have an understanding wife who will patiently bore through your afternoons of football watching, beer swilling, shouting, and having the buddies over trashing the place, while you forget to thank her for her graciousness. My wife is such. She tolerated the fact that I set up a foosball table and a stand-up arcade game in the garage, preventing us from parking the car inside so my buddies and I could spend some guy time out there drinking beer and just being guys. She drew the line at my initial suggestion that we procure a couple of neon beer signs to hang on the outside door of the garage indicating a guys' den within and my suggestion to add several more arcade games.

Though sadly without the adornment of neon, it was my own little replica of a guy's hangout, a guy's bar, if you will.

My good pal and I for some reason decided we would start a sort of contest. In the contest we alternated purchasing beers, meaning it was up to the person whose turn it was to locate a beer that neither of us had ever had before. As we began to accumulate a variety of beer bottles and caps, the idea dawned on us that the shelf that surrounded the small kitchen would be a perfect place to display the spent bottles of our findings.

While my wife was out shopping one afternoon, my friend and I emptied cardboard boxes of empty beer bottles stacked in the garage, lining the various bottles around the shelf of our kitchen, hoping she would appreciate our improvement to the dull, empty walls. There were two walls left to fill, thus our inspiration for trying even more different beers from all over the world. After building our display proudly, we grabbed a couple of bottles of beer and returned to the garage to play some more of my arcade game.

When my wife came home, we could hear her working around in the kitchen and anticipated her coming into the garage soon regarding our display; surely she would be pleased with our decorating—maybe she would have a few slight suggestions on arrangement, just adding a woman's touch of course. After a little while, she popped her head out into the garage and said, "Boys, dinner is ready" (the emphasis clearly on "boys"). We finished our game and headed in to a warm meal.

Halfway through our meal she looked at us both, a slight sympathetic smile on her face and shaking her head. She then glanced up at the shelf and asked if we could take down the beer bottles after dinner—that it was a great joke, but she had some better decorating in mind. We glanced at each other; we were quite sure she was serious but wondered how she could think our display not beautiful. We both knew better than to insist that our display of bottles with all kinds of colorful labels stay. We relegated the bottles to the garage again and within a few weeks recycled most of them; the rest we used in a display in my friend's bachelor pad, sure the right woman would come along and appreciate his interior decorating.

He was single for a lot of years.

☆

Over the next few months, my friend and I drywalled the garage, hung lights and posters, and soon the garage became the gathering place for the neighborhood teenage boys, too. Now, in addition to foosball and the arcade game, we had pinball, video games, and yes, a neon beer sign was allowed inside the garage. On any given evening, us twenty-something guys would rise to the various challenges brought by the teenage boys. Soon I was invited to rollerblade and skateboard with them in the nearby parking lots, and nearly killed myself on their skateboard ramp. I started to look for an old-fashioned pop machine for my garage "game room." After all, we were all still just boys.

My Pal Murray

Every guy should have a buddy who is just plain fun to hang around with. Someone without complicated expectations of a night out, who's easygoing and willing to laugh at themselves a bit. I feel fortunate to have a good friend like this. His name is Murray.

"There is one in every crowd." We have all said it, we have all heard it. Usually it is spoken about that person who adds a little different outlook or adds a whole new dimension to a gathering. The person who often becomes the life of the party or the sand in the oyster or both is like my Murray. Murray is all of that and more. We have known each other for several decades. Though I don't see him too often anymore because of physical distance and changes in our lives, he is still and always will be considered a lifelong dear friend, a friend who at once I feel akin to upon coming together after a long absence. He is someone with whom I've shared the sacred rights of passage, the inner secrets, the "you had to be there to get it" moments, and the long, sometimes senseless sometimes eerily philosophical conversations over a six-pack of beer.

Murray is a barrel-chested, gregarious, and very likable chap. As a matter of fact, I've never known anyone who would say one bad thing about him, but there are many who have hilarious stories to tell. Murray was a year older than the rest of us and therefore could purchase the nectar of the party prior to anyone else. This was a case for popularity in its own right back when the pursuit of a six-pack or two of beer and the attentions of a pretty member of the opposite sex were of the utmost importance.

When I was in high school, a gang of friends and I would sometimes go to the bowling ally after sharing the best part of a case of beer and roll balls toward pins in uproarious hilarity. Murray had the lightest tolerance for alcohol yet seemed to possess the greatest desire of our group to consume the largest quantity of it. By the time we got to the bowling alley he was usually three sheets to the wind already and raring to go on to the next pitcher. Murray was generally a happy-go-lucky sort. We would watch his antics in the bowling ally with great amusement; he always had a way of getting attention and often it was from the cute girls who would be watching on in curiosity.

Murray was known in high school for his old jeep, which he started with a screwdriver. He would literally padlock the jeep to the side of the school bike rack to keep the rest of us from starting it up with whatever long, hard metal object was nearby and taking it somewhere like the fifty-yard line of the school football field or to the opposing high school's front door. We'd back the jeep up the steps to the double door of the old high school building, preventing egress through it, or take it some other place where it could get its due attention. Murray never knew where he'd find his jeep next, though generally he took it all in good humor.

In the small college town in which we grew up together, there were three main attractions for young teenage boys. There was the downtown strip for cruising (to meet girls), the college campus for a variety of amusements (primarily to meet older girls), and a reservoir called Horsetooth, named after a looming rock formation that looked like two large horse teeth coming out of the mountain. A long lake sneaked back into many hidden bays, making for a great place to hold a covert party (where the girls would congregate on a weekend night).

Murray never missed a kegger party at the reservoir where most of our high school parties were held. He would flit around with a plastic cup in his hand, always telling the worst jokes but inevitably rousting a good hearty laugh from the crowd due to his delivery. He was the life of the party, sans the proverbial lampshade. During our senior year in high school, many of us would ditch classes on Fridays to go up to the reservoir for carefree late-spring afternoons of lounging on huge black inner tubes and diving off the cliffs into the water below. We often played dangerous games of "add on" and tried to impress the girls who spent time up there sunbathing. When we got low on beer, we would send the one who drew the short straw down the foothill to the nearest grocery to get another case or so of 3.2. (Usually the beer retrieval vehicle was Murray's famous jeep, whether he knew it or not.)

Large groups of teenagers would fill the sun-baked cliffs above the refreshingly cold water, music playing loudly from someone's car. The scent of suntan lotion hung in the air, and cases and cases of beer brought on the magic of summer where most of us spent every hot day whiling away the hours until the reality of summer jobs started to disburse some of us, and some would be leaving the next year to go to college. Often the majority of the crowd wouldn't leave until long after the sun had set, and sometimes the days would just work into another impromptu kegger party and bonfire.

★

There were those houses that served as the gathering places for the kids who would run in small packs. For us, it was my boyhood home and Murray's. Both our moms could cook and didn't usually mind cooking for a gang of very hungry boys. Murray's house was more centrally located, near the reservoir and not far from the other town attractions, so we usually ended up over there. His momma cooked everything in large quantities, having raised four children. Whether we were coming down from the reservoir, partying at the Library, a local watering hole, or at a friend's private party, afterward we always seemed to end up at Murray's house for a fridge raid. His momma always stocked the place with leftovers and other delicious dishes. Like an army of locusts, we would work our way through the kitchen until everything edible was consumed and then move on to the next stop, yelling our thanks and gratitude as the front door slammed shut behind us.

After high school Murray and I took an apartment together. The apartment was the source of one practical joke after another. If there was anything annoying about Murray, it was that he always operated on his own good time. He would not be rushed by the need to attend something at a certain time; more often than not I was the one waiting for him to come around. I remember one night as we were proceeding to go out and party, I had grown frustrated with him and decided to teach him a lesson. It was in the dead of winter and I used warming up my car as an excuse to set the trap. I yelled to Murray from our small kitchen that I was going out to warm up the car and that I'd be waiting in it for him. I opened and shut the front door loudly and then sneaked into our front coat closet. I stayed there totally silent for what must have been more than fifteen minutes when he came to retrieve his coat. I jumped out and screamed at the top of my lungs. He went reeling backward and vowed to pay me back, practically wetting himself. Over the course of time, practical jokes flowed back and forth making life interesting.

Not long after high school, Murray and one of our female high school friends and I moved to Austin, Texas, and took up living in an apartment there. I was there escaping a relationship gone wrong and soon came to learn that Murray had been secretly in love with my now ex-girlfriend for some time. In fact, he would anticipate her continuing love letters to me more than I did. One summer evening, he took a beer and a letter I had shrugged off as "I wish she would just get over it" and headed out to the pool just outside our door. A few minutes later our female roommate came in laughing in fits, pointing out to the pool for me to see that Murray had been so engrossed in the letter that he had fallen into the pool with his longneck brew and my love letter.

After we got back from our excursion to Texas, Murray moved back in with his parents. I went off to California, and our other roommate ended up in California, too, and became one of the famous "Bud Girls," appearing on a Budweiser poster and hopeful of more Hollywood attention.

One afternoon while in my dorm room studying, I got a call from Murray. He had been hanging Sheetrock for a living and was growing frustrated with his life. He and a work friend had apparently gone home to raid Murray's momma's famous fridge for lunch. As they settled back to watch television, a commercial caught Murray's eye. "Be all that you can be!" Something about the military services, the potential for a trade, discipline, education—whatever it was caught him up in an emotional swell he couldn't shake. Murray called the number and before he knew it had signed up for six years on board a naval ship. I imagined Murray on leave with his pals, carousing about, drinking beer, and returning to the frivolities of high school–type bonding and envied them for the time they would be spending with Murray in little taverns in Hawaii, Japan, and other exotic places their ship would sail.

Those were the days and no matter how far away those days seem, whenever I see Murray I feel like a young boy again.

Ladies Night

After all of this general discourse of male bonding and beer as the libation holding men and theirs together, it is time to tell the whole truth about beer and the vital role the womenfolk play in it. Beer is perhaps one of the oldest "foods" known to humankind, and from the beginning the making and keeping of beer was entrusted to women.

From ancient history we learn that there were an assortment of goddesses associated with beer. Nidaba was the goddess of beer in ancient Babylonia. There was Ninurta, the Babylonian goddess of wheat and barely. Nin-Bi was the goddess of beer in ancient Sumer, and let's not forget the Sumerian goddess of beer, "the lady who fills the cup," named Ninkasi. Her daughter Siris was thought of as the beer itself.

Beermaking throughout history has been entrusted to the female gender. Often the beer operations were co-located with the bread-baking operation, hence the name "liquid bread" for beer; the bread and beermaking was vital to the community and both shared similar ingredients. As societies were set up, colonies established the priorities for the new civilization, and with remarkable frequency the brew house was prominently at the top of the list. With equal emphasis the brewery or brew house or simply the brewing of beer was given great importance. One primary reason for this was sanitation and the need to assure a good drinking source, but it surely had a lot to do with the baser pleasure of beer as well.

☆

From my own experience with beer early on, it was my mother who I would tip a glass with on an otherwise lonely Friday night. It was my mother who enjoyed filling a German Pilsener with the imported golden liquid and would tell me stories of her life over a draft or two. She had come from the land of beer, Germany, and had many experiences with beer from early childhood. Long before the advent of the microbrewery and the handcrafted beers, if one wanted quality beer and variety from the usual watered-down style of American beer, it came from an imported source. The Europeans were far ahead of us in quality of the drink.

From my observation, my father was never overly particular about what beers he imbibed in. He was often willing to drink a thin, somewhat tasteless brew, mass produced and usually in a can. But my mother had a penchant for the rich German beers from her homeland, enjoying them ceremoniously in a pewter mug she had acquired in the old country. It is perhaps from her that I first learned to experiment and savor the many flavors of beer available. Interesting that my mother's taste in all things ran toward higher quality and higher prices, and ironic that my father would refer to the cliché of "champagne on a beer budget" when speaking of her proclivity to spend money. An Old Milwaukee, Coors, Hamms, or Schlitz was fine for Dad.

Once when I deviously betrayed the rules of our home regarding underage drinking, my mom pulled on me the classic psychological warfare games a parent does to entice their children to make their minds up for themselves after an overindulgence experience. The major part of the strategy was accomplished due to the simple fact that the child is no longer getting away with anything at all but that the forbidden behavior is "condoned" by the parent, thereby stripping it totally of its forbidden status. Earlier, when I was caught by a neighbor, smoking on the corner with my friends, my mother lit one cigarette after another for me to smoke, with the clear intention of making me totally lose my appetite for it. I did lose my appetite for smokes, but obviously not for beer. When I decided it was time for me to drink beer like the menfolk with some buddies in our basement and she became aware of it, it was she who set a six-pack of Dad's Old Milwaukee in front of me and commanded me to drink it down (apparently unwilling to waste the good stuff on me and somehow assuming it wouldn't be staying down anyway). Though her effort to dissuade me worked, it was short term; the only long-lasting effect her trick with the six-pack had on me was to create an aversion to Old Milwaukee beer and its unfortunate brothers. Yes indeed it made me a beer snob. But as they say, life is simply too short for bad beer.

★

Another time one of the gentler species showed well as a beer drinker was while I was in high school. We would gather at a pizza parlor called Happy Joe's on Friday nights to celebrate a victorious evening on the playing field or commiserate over a loss. One night after a football game in the late 1970s, when 3.2 beer was legal for eighteen-year-olds to consume in the pizza parlors, I watched an amusing contest between a diminutive cheerleader and a huge young man. He was one of the largest guys in our high school, weighing in at some 250 pounds, amassing much of the front line of our high school football team's offense.

He was a funny and fun-loving sort, with a reputation for the talent of being able to pour whole pitchers directly down his throat by simply tipping back his head and opening his mouth. We would buy him pitchers just to watch the feat. One night in the pizza/ice cream parlor the king of beers of our high school was challenged by several of the girls on the pompon squad to a chugging contest. He smirked chauvinistically, knowing his special talent and secret weapon would enable him to beat a man twice his size and age. Looking at the girls one half his size he took them up on their bet.

The drafts were poured, the cheerleader's own secret weapon was equipped with a tall glass, and the contest ensued. In addition to the reputation of being the undisputed beer-guzzling champion, this particular young man was known for his practical jokes and sense of humor. He was game for just about anything and everyone knew he would pay up on his debt if he were to actually lose, though no one really thought it possible. The lines were drawn, the cheering crowd parted into two factions—the guys and the gals with no dissenters.

She, too, had the uncanny talent of pouring whole glasses down her throat without the aid of swallowing more than once and had graciously turned down his offered handicap of only a two-thirds-full mug as he denoted it was only fair considering their size difference. We all stood there astonished as her glass hit the table before his.

Now, I don't remember what the other side of the bet's payoff would have been had she lost, but what I remember was that our macho, beer-swilling, football/wrestler hero was humiliated by a pompon girl. Our gladiator showed up on the next Monday donning a dress, make-up, and wig, and his own tennis shoes (for assuredly there were no pumps available to accommodate his huge feet), which he wore the entire day. I remember thinking how funny it looked to see the hulking young guy, hairy arms and legs, in a huge dress with his large tennis-shoe-clad feet sticking out beneath. He was a good sport about it, though. He took a lot of kidding, but when pushed too hard about losing to the pretty, diminutive pompon girl, he let his bulk do the talking.

☆

I also recall a beer story involving my mother-in-law—one that I threatened someday to include in a book when the time seemed right. This is dangerous territory to wade into for a writer indeed.

One thing my mother-in-law shares in common with me is a taste for good beer, though not with the same frequency or vigor (allow me a disclaimer or two to stay out of complete hot water, please). When she comes to my home for dinner, she enjoys one (or two or ...) of my varieties of beer, which change constantly because I like experimenting with new brews. I have a special place I go where a large cooler sits in the back of the store with beers that apparently have come from "broken" six-packs. I load a case or two, never the same beer twice in a case, and keep my downstairs beer fridge stocked with varieties from the darkest dark bocks and stouts to the lightest light-bodied domestics for my few lightweight friends. It is a wonderful way to discover new favorites, and it sometimes mercifully saves you from having to figure out what to do with five other beers from a six-pack you don't enjoy. But, hey, what are sporting events for but to unload those on your unsuspecting pals.

One summer night my mother- and father-in-law joined us for a barbecue at our house. I had purchased the malt beverage Zima (a whole six-pack, leaving five to pawn off on unsuspecting cronies—see what I mean about a mixed case being such a great invention?), which technically qualifies as beer, though it is clear and tastes more like Seven-Uppy wine to me. I popped the top off of one of them and handed it to my grateful mother-in-law. She immediately took to it and swigged it down as though in a race against the clock, blaming her ravenous thirst on the hot day, and asked for another (hungrily, I might add—sorry, Mom). I have known other malt beverages to carry one heck of a jolt and wondered if she knew what she was doing. I thought back on one particular night with a malt beverage favorite of my friends and me when we were first legal: Mickey's big mouths. It entailed chewing tobacco, puking, filthy jokes, an angry girlfriend, a broom, my parent's basement, and ... well, never mind, some stories are best left untold.

I considered warning her to take it slow, but at the same time I wanted to be a gracious host and thought it might be fun to see my mother-in-law three sheets to the wind. I had not yet experienced that one as of yet, so I held my tongue.

Before dinner was served, my mother-in-law had downed two of the malt beverages on an empty stomach (she claims to this day she had only two total, to this I must in the interest of truth say, "Ha!" Er ... uh, sorry again, Mom, close, but no cigar!"). As for the rest of the evening and the additional bottle count, I am sworn to secrecy. But I will tell you it could have entailed lampshades, dancing, and some drunken sailor songs and a very groggy next morning voice (well, writers do embellish a little).

To this day my mother-in-law maintains that she didn't think the beverage was alcoholic or she wouldn't have imbibed in the manner in which she did. But come on. My question is, "When did they start packaging Kool-Aid in beer bottles, Mom?" (If anyone reading this has room at the table this Christmas for a guest with no place to go, please let me know—I may need you. I'll bring the beer, or maybe there is still one bottle of the Zima left in the downstairs fridge.)

And so it goes. Beer is not just the every-man's beverage, it is indeed the every-person's beverage. So the next time you are having the in-laws or the out-laws over for a barbecue, grab a six-pack of something seemingly innocuous and watch the fun begin. Blackmail, though not legal, can still be fun.

Weekend Warriors

When you reach a certain age and stage of domesticity and the realities of your life separate you from the onetime rose-colored dreams of the adventurer or a life with no worries, you begin to ponder more of the what-could-have-beens and what-if-onlys. Everyone dreams of getting away, of living a separate life, of slipping into a persona alien to the normal, everyday routine—if only temporarily—somehow being able to strip off the conventional expectations and regain an element of the freedom once felt in youth. This feeling is often manifested in something known as a midlife crisis, but how much smarter to sample the potential change in small, weekend bites with a few buddies than diving off the deep end completely.

One of the ways a few of my friends and I retained some "freedom" was to buy Harley Davidson and Excelsior Henderson motorcycles as we tried to cling to what remained of our fleeting youth. One thing essential to riding a "Hog" is to get away from the city, the suburbs, the everyday trails and roads. To follow the road wherever it leads (so long as you're back home in time to shower and change to meet the in-laws for dinner, or something of that sort). To feel the freedom of the road, you generally find yourself in small-town America— all those "miss it if you blink" hamlets. You are able to experience for an afternoon the slow pace of people who have little interest in the hustle-bustle lifestyle that holds most of us captive most of the time.

Physical fatigue sets in after a while and you must pull over to refuel both bike and self. When I first stopped in one of these small towns to a local watering hole, I realized I was walking into a potentially rough situation. All of the preconceived notions about real bikers and real biker bars came to me as my buds and I sauntered, oh so casually, into the tough, dark place. No matter how much leather, Harley T-shirts, or other paraphernalia one wears, it is still apparent when a yuppie-type weekend warrior has entered a bona fide biker bar. All heads turned our way when we walked in; we just looked straight ahead toward the bar, not wanting to cause any trouble.

We each ordered one longneck domestic beer advertised on the bright neon signs adorning the entire length of the bar, not willing to ask the usual question, "What imports do you carry?" or, "Do you have any good microbrews on tap?" I was sitting at the long bar talking to a couple of my biker buddies who should have had emblazoned on their leather "Live to Ride, Ride to Brunch" instead of "Live to Ride, Ride to Live," when a couple of tough-looking characters sauntered in. A wrinkle-faced old-timer dressed in a biker's leather watch cap and full black leathers, complete with fringe only someone so macho could pull off without being thought of as a sissy, approached the bar. He stood there looking every bit like a bad ass Clint Eastwood in a spaghetti western or Jack Palance in *City Slickers,* asking loudly over some country singer's crooning coming from an old jukebox who it was that drove the pearl and gray Hog out front. He had an old scar across one cheek and skin so weathered I thought it must be as thick as a saddle. I could almost hear the familiar haunting warble whistle song from *The Good, the Bad, and The Ugly* ever present when the poncho-garbed, stubbed-cigarillo-chomping Eastwood appeared on screen, about to shoot the place up. His friend, who looked more like a grandpa in leathers, took a stool at the bar and watched.

As I looked around the room, something about this crowd told me that the likes of John Wayne and Clint Eastwood were the measure of a man. I eyed my friends in the mirror behind the bar and realized just how much we stuck out in there.

My mind raced as I eyed the front door and estimated how fast we could get to it, onto our bikes, and out of the parking lot if needed. He, my Clint Eastwood wannabe, may have been as old as my granddad, but he looked like he could take any man in the bar easily if it came to fisticuffs. Thoughts with lightning speed ran through my head. Did someone wipe my bike out in the parking lot? Was my Harley Davidson Nostalgia too yuppie surrounded by all of those black and chrome beauties? Was this guy a regular of this tiny tavern and had I accidentally parked in his reserved spot? I wasn't sure whether I should speak up but knew by process of quick elimination that I would be found out.

Even if I stood a fighting chance against him, it felt weird imagining getting into a bar fight at my age and even weirder considering this guy was probably thirty years older than me. (Not to mention that the regulars wouldn't likely take my side if a gang fight ensued.) All of the stereotypes about biker bars came to mind in the fleeting seconds I had while he waited for someone to respond. He asked again, this time a little too demanding, and I spoke up.

He eyed me suspiciously, came over, and sat down hard on the empty stool next to mine. My pals started to snicker, wondering what I was in for. The old guy started telling me about a police cruiser he had once owned with white walls and a two-tone paint job, much the same as mine ("except without all that newfangled computer crap they're putting on them nowadays"). To my surprise, he ordered a nonalcoholic beer.

The old fellow went on talking about the good old days when the cool bikes like Indians and Harleys looked more like mine. He slapped my leg playfully and said again, "'Course the real bikes you gotta kick start. None of that fancy-shmancy electronic start gizmo crap for me." Indeed my bike had yuppie written all over it. From the looks of his weathered hands he not only rode a real bike but also could fix anything on it, if need be. We went about covering a variety of subjects, mostly bike related, places to ride, and debated whether the ocean could possibly be as enjoyable to ride next to as the mountains were. I was on the side of the seaside ride.

After draining off the last of our suds, the old-timer invited me and my posse to join him and his posse on a ride. Two others in his bunch had already joined in. He was sure we had never been the way they were going and told us about a patch of gravel road three miles long that would take us to some of the most beautiful trout stream–side riding we'd ever see. We agreed to join them and then sped along in a pack for miles, hearing nothing but the loud verve off the tailpipes of the bikes running ahead and watched the spectacular sights in the Rocky Mountains pass by. After an hour of riding one of the more harrowing narrow roads I had ever experienced, the four old-timers pulled into a small campground, dismounted, and stretched out on some picnic tables, a part of a traditional routine, I assumed.

"This is where we nap," the Clint Eastwood lookalike scoffed. "You boys feel free to go on ahead. Loop up about five miles from here and you'll come down into a little town, or just head back the way we came." He pulled a piece of paper out of his leather jacket, a brochure with a map, and shoved it into my hands. "Feel free to bring your ladies." He walked over to the bench of the picnic table and reclined, obviously done with us for the time being. I looked at the piece of paper. It was an announcement for a pig roast that was being held later that night at a private residence I assumed to be "Clint's." It looked to have been done on a software program that drew a border of Harleys all around the map and text.

We waved back at the already nearly snoozing foursome. We opted to loop back the way we had come, wanting to assure we knew where to pick up the turnoff for future rides.

★

That evening I stood around a bonfire in back of a nice log-style home. A pig spun around a spit and a very domestic looking grandma type stepped out with two six-packs of beer, handing them around. Clint's posse stood with their wives near a roaring bonfire. I never would have recognized them as the men I had spent several hours riding with. They all looked like they had just walked off a country club golf course, and I realized they were much the same as me and my pals: weekend warriors but with many more years on the road than us. A cluster of hard-core bikers huddled around the turning pig and eyed us newcomers somewhat suspiciously. But by the end of the evening we had all mixed together, little difference between most of us, save our daily lifestyles.

We soon came to discover that the sweet-looking grandma type was Clint's wife of thirty-some-odd years. The now clean-shaven, tall, salt-and-pepper-bearded Clint Eastwood lookalike biker was actually a retired physicist and had taught science at a university before retiring to his foothills dream house, biking and building fine wood furniture and playing around on his computer. The house he lived in and the woman he lived with were a stark contrast from the impression we had gotten of the man with whom we had spent the afternoon tooling around. As he showed me through the unique house, we looked over some black and white photographs of his earlier days, several of him and some friends on the back of the police-type bikes that first brought us to conversation. We looked at his workbench and "playroom" where he and his buddies played pool and cards. I spotted an old-fashioned phonograph in the corner and a large selection of classical music.

A few weeks later we ran into Clint and his posse in the same little biker bar again. As if on cue we all stood, walked out, and searched for another hidden trout stream to ride beside. We rode through the magestic Rocky Mountains in a pack, passing rivers, farms, meadows, and other sights that can be appreciated in a unique way when on a motorcycle. We again parted ways when Clint and his friends decided to take a siesta.

Though that was the last time we rode with Clint, we have picked up a ride here and there with other small packs. I learned growing up not to judge a book by its cover or a person by their outward appearance. I am glad the bikers we have palled around with learned it, too.

You Can Never Go Home Again

As I pulled into my hometown for my twenty-year high school reunion, I realized I was a stranger returning to a place I had once called home but which had changed as much as I had since I left it. Like many others who have moved away from a small town to find their way in the expansive world beyond, I remember the boy thinking of the cow town I forever wanted to separate myself from. I would learn later that no matter where I went, the boy who remained inside longed somehow to return to that simple, familiar place.

I drove the southern route into my hometown past my once country boyhood home, now surrounded by modern commerce; the predictions made so long ago about the two nearby towns someday connecting had virtually come true. What once was a small country setting was now disheartening-ly a row of big box stores, auto dealerships, and furniture stores that lined the widened highway. Disoriented by the new look of the place, I made several wrong turns on what once was very familiar territory. Like the changing landscape of my hometown, there would be many changes in the old school chums I would soon encounter.

We convened the first night of the weekend reunion at a tavern that many of us had frequented in high school. A group of people, mostly strangers now, gathered in the smoky den and began to sip from kegged beers as we had two decades earlier. Each person silently judging how kind time had been to them in comparison to the peers of yesteryear or the other way around.

I had heard of stories by friends who had already attended their twenty-year reunion and wondered if my class would fall into the same cliché, where the guys mostly would have beer bellies, balding heads, compensating cars, and over-inflated stories of great successes. Would the women, most of whom had childbearing behind them and who had looked a little rougher around the edges at the ten-year reunion, look more as they had in high school, with of course the exception of increased wisdom and street smarts?

I scanned the crowd for familiar faces, but what I found instead were the resemblances of some of my one-time friends' *parents*. Then I realized the inconceivable. Today we had all become closer to the age our parents were when we were school kids. The fact that the faces of my peers were now closer reflections to what their parents had looked like shouldn't have come as such a surprise, but somehow in my mind my school chums had stopped aging some twenty years ago. Now the mirror was sharpening. We were all creeping on, and for the first time I really tangibly grasped how fast time slips by.

I looked around for the face of one of my best friends in high school. Even though I knew he had passed away, he belonged there among us. The last time I had seen him was at our ten-year reunion. It seemed odd to think that one of us was gone, then rumors began to trickle through the crowd of others who had met untimely deaths. As though instinctually, we all lifted more than one mug of beer to our fallen comrades and laughed as we remembered our favorite high school class clown who once downed whole pitchers in one long pour down his throat. We lifted our mugs to our own mortality, and somehow the beer tasted sweeter being there in the same dark tavern we had once drunk in. Some of us had used fake IDs back then and were more intent to put on a buzz while the months drew nearer to our supposed freedom brought on by graduation.

I thought of the people sitting on the very stools we now sat perched on, changed by much in the two decades since. There I had drowned my sorrows with some empathetic friends after being dumped by a girl I had considered many times dropping myself, but somehow the fact that she had dropped me made me want her back so bad it had ached. The only logical way to assuage the pain was to find solace in some rowdy companionship and a few too many brewskies. Now several old chums described their first and failed marriages and the hardships of their relationships, not altogether that different from the reports of our women friends..

We recounted our youthful mischief and laughed at so many of the shared memories we had taken with us over the years. Memories were dredged up for those who had spent the past two decades earnestly trying to forget their part in the antics. The common, carefree recollections cheered those of us who had just begun to feel as though we were getting old. New stories were added as we swapped tales of contemporary friendships and of how much our lives had indeed changed. Some of us picked up with each other as though no time had passed at all, and some resorted to "Wow, it's been so long!" and "You haven't changed a bit." Yet all of us wrestled with how to answer the question "So what have you been up to?"

We mingled about with a beer in one hand and a constant handshake in the other. I laughed to myself thinking how interesting it was that most of us were nursing our beers and wines slowly to keep our conversations intelligent in the same place where the goal had often been to pound down as many as we could in the shortest time possible with little thought to the conversation.

The evening that had begun with somewhat reserved decorum (after all, we were not kids anymore—most of us were parents and responsible members of society) began to loosen a little more with each passing hour. As the beers increased in frequency, the decorative helium balloons came down, and some of the old high school antics began again. Grown men with responsibilities, families, and reputations began to suck down the helium in the balloons, providing the ridiculous Donald Duck voice that made others roar with laughter as some of the women looked on with the same amazed disbelief they had felt with these lads in high school—most glad that they hadn't married the boy next door.

Some of the "adult" protocol we all had felt at the beginning of the evening slipped into memory as we once again toasted our remaining youth and recounted more funny stories from a time that now seemed borrowed from another's life. The next day I heard that the heartiest celebrators in the crowd I had left shortly after midnight had moved the party to someone's parents' house as we had done two decades ago. Those who continued to drink beer early into the next day were absent from the morning activities as they had been absent from first-period classes back in school.

Though much of the landscape and the circumstances we had found ourselves in two decades later were different, much remained the same. Time hadn't changed us that much after all, really.

While on My Porch

One unseasonably warm spring evening, the sunset casting orange across the entire sky, my nine-year-old-going-on-eighteen-year-old son and I shot baskets, played some one-on-one and a few games of "Pig," "Horse," and "Twenty-one" until we were both sweating and tired (actually a nine-year-old boy will never claim tired). As I propped myself up, reclining on my elbows on the front porch, I asked him to go into the house and pick out a special beer for me to cut the thirst from my overexertion. Whatever looked good to him would be fine with me. I hoped somehow he would make the correlation between athletically earned thirst and something relatively light-bodied, noncomplicated, rather than a thick, syrupy, hoppy brew that I might better enjoy with a juicy steak and with less need for the immediate quenching of thirst.

Often sending a boy to do a man's job is a dicey proposition, particularly when your basement fridge contains at any given time somewhere between twenty-four to forty-eight different beers. When a light ale or amber would refresh and he might bring out a Guinness or some other stout, still I would never ask him to go back in and pick again. He enjoys controlling that much of my destiny anyway. The fact that he has been through this routine before has educated him to bring a church key along with him. There's one hanging off my workbench in the garage and one in the glove compartment of my car for that spur-of-the-moment, going-to-the-park, pick-up-a-"sixer" to share time, or for the summer camping trip when inevitably the church key is left behind and someone feels compelled to prove that indeed they can still remove a bottle cap from a beer with their teeth.

He returned to the front porch, where I sat a little more exhausted than I was willing to let on, with two bottles and a church key, to which I remarked, "Very funny little man—two, huh?" affectionately rubbing the top of his head.

"Mom said I could have it," he replied, and turned to show me the "near beer," the nonalcoholic brew in a longneck bottle, similar to the mercifully light-bodied German-style Hefeweizen he had brought for me. (Yes! They can learn.) I raised my eyebrow, to which he said, "Ask Mom!" as though I, his father, had absolutely no authority or say-so in the matter. So, just to be sure, I stood and went to the front door, holding it open and called in to ask if it was really okay with her if he had the near beer.

After playfully grumbling about me bellowing throughout the entire house, her needing to come to the front to hear me, she gave me one of those looks that says more than words ever could and nodded. "Just this once!" she insisted. Then I saw what looked like a curling smile forming on her face as she realized he and I were bonding out there.

My son stood on the porch, beaming at me with an "I told you so" look, thinking of his own right of passage and anticipating his own "beer" with good old dad. I thought back to the day on the roof of my childhood home, when I looked down, watching the menfolk of my community kevetching and carrying on while sipping from the bottles of the mysteriously bitter, golden amber and wanting so much to be like them. How is it that when we are young, all we want to do is to grow older and be able to do the things that we think look so cool? How when the sands of time pour through and we look up to find that our childhood is far behind us, we long for the care-free days of youth again? We're never satisfied with the age and stage we hold, always looking forward or backward. I remember my need to feel like I was one of the guys and realized it had all come full circle on my porch with my younger son.

I held my bottle out, motioning to him to do the same and said, "Okay then, little man, you do the honors." He popped the tops off, we clinked bottles, and both sat on the front porch watching another day end as the sun now gone retreated behind the mountains west of our house. We sipped side by side from our bottles of suds and talked about nothing in particular, yet somehow we were communicating wonderfully.

My other son pulled up into the driveway on his bike, looked at the two of us sitting side by side on the porch step tipping back longneck bottles with curiosity and what I sensed to be slight envy. His younger brother, my current drinking buddy, let out a very satisfied "Ah!" and tauntingly held the bottle up for all to see that he had already drunk half of it. Then my older son rolled his eyes, shook his head in disbelief, and headed into the house with an "I'm telling Mom!" Again my authority was under question. I shrugged it off and pulled a long, satisfying drink from the wheat beer.

I thought to myself that my little man was growing up and in no time would be off on his own. I looked at his face as he proudly sipped from his bottle like a grown-up, like dad, now giving off an exaggerated "Ahhh!"' with every sip and relishing every drop of his little rite of passage. I told him that the children in Europe, specifically in Germany, started drinking real beer when they were quite young, a part of the culture.

He looked at me and said, "Cool."

I pulled the last off the bottom of my refreshing Hefeweizen, slapped his leg, and asked, "You up for another game of Horse?" as I rolled the basketball under my extended foot. He looked at me and said, "Nah, Dad, I've had a long day, I think I will just relax and have a brewski."

Where had he heard that I wondered and suppressed a grin. How far things have come. From my first stolen beer on my parents' house rooftop, to my front porch, where my sons can share the stolen moments with their dad. Though not quite the same experience, it is truly a right of passage. Just then, my older son came bounding out onto the porch, holding his own near beer. I smiled, looked at him sitting next to his little brother, rolled him the basketball, which he stopped expertly with his foot like a soccer ball, and said, "Not yet little buddy ol' pal. Not till you've earned it!" and we both headed for the hoop.

I looked from our driveway makeshift basketball court to the split in the eaves of our roof. I thought that maybe later I might show the boys how to remove the screen on the window leading to the flat part of our roof where they could climb up to the point where they would have a view of all of the fireworks displays that played across the sky from the numerous suburbs surrounding us on the Fourth of July. Life viewed from a rooftop is a good one indeed. Ah, the simple independent moments of life, the stolen memory building moments that define much of our reason for toiling as hard as we do. For as the old saying goes, all work and no play makes Jack a dull boy. Lift a glass to those days of independence!

About the Author

Justin Matott lives with his family in Colorado. He is the best-selling author of two books of essays, and several children's books. When he is not writing he is reading; when he is not reading, he is an avid skier, snowshoer, runner, biker, hiker, traveler, and Olympic-potential twelve-ounce curler. Sometimes he remembers to smell the flowers.

Since he was a young boy, Matott has been entertaining friends and family with his imaginative storytelling. It was only when he realized that he was repeating his stories too often that he began to write them down. He continues to write ceaselessly.